KIRK

Teaching Success Guide for the Advanced Placement Classroom

KIRK

Advanced Placement Classroom

Lord of the Flies

Advanced Placement Classroom

Lord of the Flies

Timothy J. Duggan, Ed.D.

PRUFROCK PRESS INC.
WACO, TEXAS

Library of Congress Cataloging-in-Publication Data

Duggan, Timothy J.
 Lord of the Flies / by Timothy J. Duggan, Ed.D.
     pages cm. -- (Teaching Success Guide for the Advanced Placement Classroom)
 Includes bibliographical references.
 ISBN 978-1-61821-030-2 (pbk.)
 1. Golding, William, 1911-1993. Lord of the flies. 2. Golding, William, 1911-1993--Study and teaching (Higher) I. Title.
 PR6013.O35L6328 2013
 823'.914--dc23
                    2013000204

Edited by Sean Redmond
ISBN: 978-1-61821-030-2

At the time of this book's publication, all facts and figures cited are the most current available. All telephone numbers, addresses, and website URLs are accurate and active. All publications, organizations, websites, and other resources exist as described in the book, and all have been verified. The author and Prufrock Press Inc. make no warranty or guarantee concerning the information and materials given out by organizations or content found at websites, and we are not responsible for any changes that occur after this book's publication. If you find an error, please contact Prufrock Press Inc.

•AP and Advanced Placement Program are registered trademarks of the College Entrance Examination Board, which was not involved in the production of, and does not endorse, this book.

Prufrock Press Inc.
P.O. Box 8813
Waco, TX 76714-8813
Phone: (800) 998-2208
Fax: (800) 240-0333
http://www.prufrock.com

To my brother, Mike, and my sister, Erin,
for allowing me to survive childhood.

Contents

Acknowledgments

I would like to thank my graduate students at Northeastern Illinois University for the time we have spent discussing *Lord of the Flies*. I thank my department chair, Brian Schultz, and my colleagues at Northeastern, especially Katy Smith, René Luis Alvarez, Tim Scherman, Tim Libretti, Anna Antaramian, Jim Blair, and Cyndi Moran for discussions about teaching and writing. I thank my editor at Prufrock Press, Sean Redmond, for keeping me on track and for his valuable feedback.

I thank the members and leaders of the National Council of Teachers of English and the Illinois Association of Teachers of English for creating outstanding national and state professional communities and for allowing me to try out my ideas on an audience of peers. I thank my colleagues Marilyn Halperin of the Chicago Shakespeare Theatre, Mary Massie of the Chicago Teachers Center, Christian Hewalt, Ryan Dooley, Alison Morales, and Sergio Santillan. Thanks to the faculty and administration at Roald Amundsen High School in Chicago.

Thanks to Toodie Duggan for asking me "How's the book going?" and to Mike Duggan and Erin Pemberton for moral support in absentia. Finally, I thank my wife, Heidi Nickisch Duggan, and my two children, Eamon and Liesel.

"Aren't there any grownups at all?": Introduction

Welcome to *Advanced Placement Classroom*: Lord of the Flies. If you have purchased this book, I can assume that you are about to embark on a literary journey to an uncharted tropical island, and you are interested in reinforcing your own ideas with other possibilities to create a valuable learning experience for your students. I hope and trust that you will find classroom activities here that will enhance the journey. How you use the book will be entirely up to you, as my own approach has been to generate a number of ideas, to contextualize and describe those ideas in clear language so that you can reproduce them as you see fit, and to align those activities to standards-based learning objectives.

Lord of the Flies is a cautionary tale. If we don't see it as such, there may not be much point in reading it, other than to marvel at the writing itself or to depress ourselves with the notion that humanity is doomed by its own bestial nature. I don't believe that to be true, and although Golding commented publicly that his desire was to "trace the defects in the characters back to the defects in man's nature" (qtd. in Epstein, p. 238), I do not think everyone interpreted Golding's statement accurately. Golding could not give us this masterpiece and the subsequent brilliant novels he produced if he thought there was no hope for humanity. He couldn't have produced a luminous character like Simon, a baffled but decent boy like Ralph, an intelligent but bullied individual like Piggy, or a troubled and addictive personality like Jack if he thought there was no hope for them to make the right decisions and thrive in their troublesome situation. But of course, these fictional boys do not make the right decisions in the text and, thus, things do not work out so well for them. It is we, the readers, who are left to piece out what might have been different and what Golding's parable (or fable, or myth) means for us.

My own desire to write this book connects to my experience teaching it to high school students and training preservice teachers to teach it in their own secondary English classrooms. The story and the characters last in one's imagination long after the reading experience itself. One reads this story with the sort of horrible fascination that one feels watching tragedy on the theatre stage. The story's main characters have become modern archetypes of the personalities they represent, and there are plenty of situations that arise in the story that allow us to discuss with our students concepts of empathy, democracy, shared responsibility, discretion, and cooperation. The book is also remarkably contemporary. Although readings that connect the book to the "darkness of man's heart" and that examine the function of order and society in opposition to nature and wildness have been around for decades, the book finds new currency in our concerns about bullying in schools, our preoccupation with conflicts that arise in reality television shows like *Survivor*, and our ongoing examination of our relationship with (and potential destruction of) nature.

Reading as Experience

Reading *Lord of the Flies* or any other serious novel within the context of a school classroom constitutes an educational experience, and, as teachers, we design that educational experience for our students. What they actually experience cannot be exactly what we imagine or design, but our influence is enormous and may dictate whether their encounter with the text is beneficial or boring. John Dewey (1938) claimed that the best sort of educational experience was the one that led the learner to want to have another, similar experience. In other words, we can never assess our success solely on what our students do at the time they encounter the work under study. We will need to look ahead to subsequent behaviors to see whether reading and studying *Lord of the Flies* has made our students more or less willing to pursue new encounters with difficult novels.

A friend of mine who teaches English found out that I was writing this book, and he sent me an e-mail that said:

> Don't forget to include the fact that Samneric represent the interchange-able, gullible common man who is stupidly attracted to the superficial qualities of evil ("Can we wear paint, too?") and weakly cowed by evil's brutal power ("We have to go, Roger is coming.") They also let the civilization signal die out so they can run around and poke pigs with sticks. (Johnny Knoxville, anyone?) (C. Hewalt, personal communication, September 13, 2012)

I admire the critical acumen of my colleague and friend, and his comment demonstrates how strongly many teachers feel about the lessons to be learned from Golding's novel. But his setup implies that I as the teacher should give my students an interpretation that he considers vital to the overall meaning of the book. And this is precisely what I encourage you to think about in your own teaching. I would love for my students to generate an interpretive statement like the one above on their own, but if I give that statement or that interpretation to them, then they have little or no stake in it. They are only witnessing my (or in this case, my friend's) interpretive skill. As Louise Rosenblatt (Blau, 2003) stated, taking someone else's interpretation as your own is like having someone eat your dinner for you. One of the most difficult things for English teachers to do is refrain from burdening students with our well-trained readings of cherished texts. What we often do is take a Socratic approach and design questioning sessions that ultimately lead to the interpretations we value, such as "What about Samneric?" . . . "Are they interchangeable?" . . . "How responsible are they?" . . . and so on, until students eventually arrive at our interpretation or retreat entirely from the process, leaving us to answer our own questions. I hope to offer productive classroom discussion tips that will lead students to take a stake in their interpretations without coercion, while allowing teachers to share their thoughts as well.

We may also hope that our students will develop a positive stance toward the book so that they may encounter it at a later time and eagerly dive back into the story with whatever perspectives they have gained in the intervening years of their lives. We cannot give our students a comprehensive experience with the book, nor should we attempt such a feat. Such is true with any great literature in the classroom, from Shakespeare to Golding. Our students cannot explore every possible reading of the book, and many teachers make the mistake of loading the students down with every symbol, every metaphor, and every interpretation, which leaves nothing for later discovery and overwhelms even the most gifted readers. We can teach them to encounter the text with determination and rigor, with the understanding that the book offers deeper treasures for future readings. As a teacher, you may have productive, engaging discussions and readings with your students, leading to their production of complex and reasonable writing or project work. This book offers ideas to support preparation for reading, the initial encounters with the text, and follow-up study and student work.

Reading a Text Versus Studying a Text

We must acknowledge that, in the classroom, students don't simply read for pleasure, and so merely reading *Lord of the Flies* is not sufficient for your lesson designs. Many teachers are so happy when they have success getting students to do one simple reading of a text that they forget the point of rereading, of probing, of taking bits and pieces of the text and poring over them over and over to build an interpretation. They forget the value of examining secondary informative and argumentative texts to spark discussion of themes and other literary elements. The activities and potential assignments described in this book will help your students to systematically read, think about, discuss, and write about the book in ways that open up analysis and build their confidence.

Part of studying texts is also the building of a literary vocabulary and a familiarity with the processes and language associated with literary analysis and criticism. *Lord of the Flies* offers students an example of a novel that fully engages the traditional literary elements, and while you as the teacher may be introducing or reinforcing your students' understanding of literary terms like "symbolism" or "setting" through their study of *Lord of the Flies*, the greater benefit of using this book will be to make the language of literary elements and devices operational for the students. In other words, it is not enough to use the examples in the novel to teach about symbolism or irony or setting—students must own those terms by using them appropriately, something the activities in this book will encourage and develop.

In this era of instant access, students can easily find a large number of prefabricated readings of the text. I believe that students should always encounter literature first from an open intellectual space, as opposed to seeing a work first through the eyes of another's analysis. That said, the study of a work of literature should never end with one's personal and often naïve stance. For that reason, we will look at a number of critical sources (see Chapter 6) to further our study of the book.

The Book, Historically

When Golding's novel first appeared in 1954, it did not make much of a splash (Carey, 2009), but by the early 1960s, the book had replaced Salinger's *Catcher in the Rye* as the most popular book on college campuses (*Time*, 1962). It has enjoyed a steady readership and popularity ever since, and it has become a staple in the canon of required school texts in English classes. It also continues to appear on syllabi for college courses in everything from modern literature to sociology to political science. While most Golding scholars consider either *Pincher Martin* (1956) or *The Spire* (1964) to be his masterpiece, *Lord of the Flies* continues to be Golding's most popular and culturally pervasive work. The book and its author have engendered so much criticism and analysis among the academy that Golding himself felt compelled to jump into the fray and explain the work on several occasions (e.g., Biles, 1970), and Golding eventually wrote a fictional parody of the relationship between a writer and his literary biographer in *The Paper Men* (1984).

Although Harold Bloom (2008) dismissed *Lord of the Flies* as a period piece, wedded to the post-World War II era that produced it, the book continues to haunt readers and students. Perhaps the book remains in school curricula not only due to its use of established literary elements, such as symbol, but because it is both accessible and challenging to young readers. Another reason to teach the book is that the new Common Core State Standards clarify goals for literacy education and emphasize encounters with complex fictional and informational texts. *Lord of the Flies* and its accompanying volume of critical analysis provide the balance between literary and informational text that the Common Core advocates.

Common Core State Standards

The Common Core State Standards articulate a vision for college and career readiness across core subjects in primary and secondary school curricula. Developed by a partnership between the National Governor's Association and school reform groups such as Achieve, Inc., the standards shift the focus of literacy away from discrete individual skills toward higher level competencies across domains of reading, writing, speaking, listening, and language. The standards are stated and explained on the Common Core website at http://www.corestandards. org/ELA-Literacy/CCRA/R.

The Common Core State Standards for grades K–12 reading consist of 10 anchor standards split among four areas of concern for both literary and informational texts. The first three standards are listed under the heading "Key Ideas and Details" and concern themselves with the practice of close reading (including explicit decoding and inference making), citing evidence in text to support an interpretation, and tracing development of characters, ideas, and themes throughout a text. The second heading is "Craft and Structure," and these standards focus on specific textual elements such as vocabulary, literal and figurative meaning, text structure, and point of view. The third heading is "Integration of Knowledge and Ideas." Contained here are competencies in comparing texts, analyzing textual ideas in broader contexts, and considering the connection between genre and meaning. Finally, "Range of Reading and Level of Text Complexity" (Standard 10) addresses the goal of developing students' ability to read both literary and informational texts of increasing complexity with increasing independence. Specific benchmarks for how these competencies are manifested through assessment at different grade levels are stated under the separate tabs of "Literature" and "Informational Text."

A similar approach has been taken for the Common Core State Standards for writing, speaking and listening, and language. Headings have been constructed for each, with stated standards distributed underneath and specific grade-level benchmarks provided. I encourage you to familiarize yourself with these standards as soon as possible, even if your state and district have not implemented them, as they are driving much of the new textbook and curriculum material being created today.

In this book, I identify the connection between specific activities and Common Core State Standards using the signification labels of the Common Core State Standards Initiative (see the website cited above). For example, if an activity aligns to Reading Literature Standard 1 at the 11–12 level, I have labeled it CC RL.11-12.1, which matches the labeling used. I have used benchmarks from the 11–12 grade level, as this is when students typically take AP classes, but I have also included standards from the 9–10 grade level, as *Lord of the Flies* is commonly taught at these grades as well. Note that, because the standards are spiral, many of the activities presented here are appropriate for use with a wide range of levels.

AP Writing

Lord of the Flies is an excellent book to use to prepare students for AP writing tasks. The book's presentation of symbols, the powerful function of setting (not just physical, but also psychological), the fully drawn characters, and the imagery all fit well with the AP focus for free-response essays. Chapter 6 will examine model prompts related to the book that mimic AP free-response and text-based questions.

Structure of This Book

This book is structured to help you prepare for and execute a successful unit that employs *Lord of the Flies* as either the central text or as a representative text in a multitext unit related to a larger theme, such as war, power, or the function of rules, just to name a few possibilities. *Lord of the Flies* may serve you well by stimulating discussion, sparking research, and connecting to other texts, or it can stand alone as a text offering opportunities for deep and enduring learning.

Chapter 2 takes a look at the book as it has been interpreted by others and introduces aspects of Golding's life and work. It also describes the characters in some detail and includes a plot summary.

Chapter 3 takes us directly into the teaching process by introducing a series of prereading activities designed to engage students and increase their curiosity about the book. My hope is that by the end of Chapter 3 you will be ready to dive into the text yourself, even if you are still preparing to take your students along.

Chapter 4, the longest chapter in the book, is a scene-by-scene reading guide. As my premise, I imagine you and I preparing to team-teach the text and reading it together, perhaps days or weeks before the beginning of the unit. I share my thoughts as we read together every section of every chapter from beginning to end. This read-along is interspersed with discussion and journal activities to help students process their initial reading of the book.

Chapter 5 includes postreading discussions and performance ideas that lead students back into the text through structured debates, reader's theatre, and additional multilevel discussion topics for each chapter. The goal is to get students to take responsibility for driving discussion of the book and for developing individual and shared interpretations.

Chapter 6 presents writing topics for each stage of the students' encounter with the novel, including informal process writing, character interventions, summary news reports, and model AP prompts for writing about the book. Creative writing ideas are shared at the end.

Chapter 7 presents project ideas for students to explore as follow-ups to their initial reading. A number of discrete project ideas are presented and explained, with possible resources identified to help students with each. I highly recommend using Chapter 7 to create small-group investigations leading to a large, whole-class sharing that will deepen and broaden students' overall experience with *Lord of the Flies*.

Chapter 8 in this book will list some additional resources related to *Lord of the Flies*. So much has been written about Golding's first novel that it may seem absurd to add yet another book to the pile of available teaching guides, critical commentaries, and textual analyses. During the preparation for writing this book, I looked at many of those guides, essays, and analyses, and I can assure you that you would need a 50-year sabbatical to get through all of them. But many scholars and teachers have developed great ideas about the text and about ways to address it in the classroom, and I encourage you to diversify your preparation by looking at some of these materials.

A Note on Students and Reading

You know your students better than I do, so you know what specific challenges you will face in working through the novel with them. Getting them to read the book, page by page, front to back, and then to exercise a willingness to take another look, to pore over specific passages and to tease out an interpretation—that is your essential challenge. Be aware that any student today has access to numerous synopses and interpretations via the Internet, from CliffsNotes to SparkNotes to Shmoop and hundreds of other sources. If you merely assign students to read on their own and then do traditional recitation questioning in class the following day, you are likely to get students who know plenty about the chapters without ever having read them. The relationship you develop with your students will help determine how much integrity they exhibit in completing assignments and experiencing the novel, and I strongly encourage you to cultivate an atmosphere of cooperation and shared learning from the beginning of your unit. A possible unit structure appears below.

Possible Structure of a Unit

Whenever we embark on a teaching unit, we need to consider what we want to accomplish, which means we have to consider what knowledge, skills, and deeper understandings we want our students to demonstrate and take away from the unit. We also need to think about dispositions toward future literary study we want to nurture through the day-to-day work of the unit. A rough outline of a unit might look like this:

Week 1:   Set out goals and structure for unit.
          Orientation and prereading activities (Chapter 3).
          Begin reading in class.

Week 2:   Continue reading with supplemental activities (Chapters 4, 5, and 6).

Week 3:   Finish initial reading of text.
          Engage discussion, performance, and writing (Chapters 5 and 6).
          Engage secondary sources (Chapter 6).
          Form teams for project work (Chapter 7).

Week 4:   Writing assessments (Chapter 6) and team work on projects (Chapter 7).

Week 5:   Students present projects (Chapter 7).
          Shared reflection and assessment of learning.

"Come on, we're explorers": Teaching *Lord of the Flies*

When choosing novels for the classroom, teachers have several considerations to make. How long is the book? How will it fit with the rest of the curriculum? Will it be featured as the core of the unit, or will it be a component in a larger thematic unit that addresses a number of core standards? How will it challenge students, yet not frustrate their interpretive efforts? *Lord of the Flies* is a staple in school curricula because it is at once accessible and difficult, engaging and philosophical. This chapter covers some background on the book and its author, gives a short review of critical stances, introduces the characters, and includes a brief plot summary.

William Golding's Life and Work

William Golding was born in 1911 in Cornwall, England, and he died in 1993. According to the Nobel Prize series (1993), his father was a schoolmaster and his mother was a suffragette. He studied science at Oxford University but grew disillusioned with his studies and defected to English literature. After five years at Oxford, he published a short volume of poems in 1935. In 1939 he began teaching at Bishop Wordsworth's School in Salisbury, but left in 1940 to join the Royal Navy. He saw action in World War II, which affected his views on human nature (Golding, 1982), and he reached the rank of lieutenant. After the war he returned to teaching, and it wasn't until he was well established as a writer with four books in print that he quit his teaching job. He enjoyed a long career, receiving the Nobel Prize for Literature in 1983. Although *Lord of the Flies* is not usually considered his masterwork, it remains his most popular work. His second novel, *The Inheritors* (1955), and his third novel, *Pincher Martin* (1956), continued the exploration into the nature of humanity's basic flaws that he began with *Lord of the Flies*. Those books also have structural similarities, most notably the reversal of narrative perspective at the end. Later works include the novels *Free Fall* (1959), *The Spire* (1964), *The Pyramid* (1967), *Darkness Visible* (1979), *The Paper Men* (1984), and the *To the Ends of the Earth* trilogy, made up of *Rites of Passage* (1980), *Close Quarters* (1987), and *Fire Down Below (1989)*. He also published *The Brass Butterfly* (a play, 1958), *The Hot Gates* (essays, 1965), *The Scorpion God* (three novellas, 1971), *A Moving Target* (essays and autobiographical pieces, 1982), and *An Egyptian Journal* (a travel log, 1985).

In a recent biography, John Carey (2009) shared in great detail the story of Golding's struggle to get a publisher interested in his manuscript for *Lord of the Flies*, which first bore the title "Strangers from Within." It was the lucky circumstance of having the book fall into the hands of Charles Monteith, an editor just starting out at the Faber and Faber publishing house in London, which led to the publication of *Lord of the Flies*. The book sold moderately at first, but by 1962 it was immensely popular in America (*Time,* 1962). Golding and Monteith enjoyed a long and productive professional relationship and friendship until Golding's death.

What Is This Book About?

On its face, *Lord of the Flies* is an adventure story of boys at some undetermined time in history or in the future who are evacuated from a nuclear conflict and ejected onto a tropical, uninhabited island. The story traces their conflicts as they struggle to organize their society and facilitate their rescue. As time goes by, the boys split into factions, and the brutal faction that is interested in hunting achieves dominance over the civil faction that functions through parliamentary procedures. The boys become savages, eventually hunting and killing each other.

As we will see from the perspectives of a handful of scholars, the book is about much more than adventure. The book has been critiqued and written about extensively for the past 50 years, so it would not be possible or productive to attempt a comprehensive survey of the critical literature. However, a sampling of secondary sources can offer us a taste of the conversations that have gone on over time and give us a sense of the book's place in contemporary culture.

In his critical note in the Riverhead edition of the text (which was used in the preparation of this book), E. L. Epstein quotes Golding as having stated the following:

> The theme is an attempt to trace the defects in society back to the defects of human nature. The moral is that the shape of a society must depend

on the ethical nature of the individual and not on any political system however apparently logical or respectable. The whole book is symbolic in nature except the rescue in the end where adult life appears, dignified and capable, but in reality enmeshed in the same evil as the symbolic life of the children on the island. The officer, having interrupted a man-hunt, prepares to take the children off the island in a cruiser which will presently be hunting its enemy in the same implacable way. And who will rescue the adult and his cruiser? (p. 238)

Many critics have used the words of the author in interviews and subsequent writings to reinforce their interpretations. Epstein focuses on what he describes as Golding's "superb use of symbolism" (p. 239). He discusses the Lord of the Flies as the central symbol: a literal translation of Beelzebub, the name "suggests that he is devoted to decay, destruction, demoralization, hysteria and panic" (p. 239). Epstein sees this devil more akin to the Freudian id than to a religious symbol; it is more amoral than immoral and can be found in much of modern literature. He uses the sexually explicit killing of the sow and Simon's interview with the pig's head as the central scenes connecting the boys to a nature that is "blackness" and "insatiable" (p. 242).

Similar to Epstein, Johnston (1980) described the novel in connection to Golding's statements on the defective nature in man, demonstrating how Golding "intrudes" on the text at certain points to make the message obvious, such as at the assembly, when Simon says of the beast, "maybe it's only us" (p. 98). Indeed, Golding had several opportunities to explain the book during his career. At one point, reflecting on the lessons learned from World War II, he claimed that the theme of the book is "grief, sheer grief, grief, grief, grief" (Golding, 1982, p. 163).

Baker (1963) also connected the book's themes to basic human nature, describing the influence of *The Bacchae* by Euripides on Golding. In *The Bacchae*, Pentheus is destroyed not because the followers of Bacchus are naturally evil, but because Pentheus seeks to repress the wild, chaotic pleasure principle. Baker rejected a strictly symbolic reading of the book, stating that although the book parallels the myth of Pentheus as represented in *The Bacchae*, the boys on the island ultimately are just boys who want to be rescued (or who don't think about rescue). Golding's achievement is to give them symbolic stature while filling them with enough real personality to prevent our seeing them merely as symbols (Kinkead-Weekes & Gregor, 1967; Tiger, 1974). Extending this play between symbolic and nonsymbolic reading, we can say that the objects on the island also resist being merely symbolic (Delbaere-Garant, 1978; Sugimura, 2008). Ultimately, the pig's head is not a symbol, it is a "pig's head on a stick," as Simon says (p. 164), and the conch is just a conch.

But the book also has a spiritual element to it, mainly channeled through Simon. Simon has been juxtaposed against Roger as good versus evil (Olsen, 2000) and more often against Piggy as the mystical versus the rational or the intuitive versus the intellectual. Golding's preference for the mystical over the rational is summed up in Johnston's (1980) analysis of the deaths of Simon and Piggy: "whereas Simon is described in language befitting a dead saint, Piggy is pictured as a dead animal" (p. 16). Many writers have focused on Simon as the preferred character to Piggy, and Golding himself mentioned that Ralph should be weeping for Simon rather than Piggy at the end of the book (Biles, 1970, p. 12). Delbaere-Garant (1978) further explored the symbolic differences in Simon and Piggy, seeing Simon as a representation of the passive, intuitive, and spiritual side of nature, whereas Piggy is rational and determined to change the world. Like Johnston, she pointed to the significant differences in the descriptions of their deaths as indicative of those two sides of human nature. For Delbaere-Garant, the novel does not differentiate between the nature of man and nature itself—man is only an extension. The boys' retreat from civilization, represented by assemblies and expeditions, into the irrational side of nature is exemplified by "throwing rocks and killing pigs" (Delbaere-Garant, 1978, p. 77). Whereas the boys progress from throwing rocks to rolling large stones that kill, the adult world is symbolized by the atomic bomb—a very large rock, indeed.

The main struggle in the book, however, is not between Simon and Piggy, who are tentative allies, but between Ralph and Jack, the two competing leaders. The main characters have been associated with a variety of allegorical analogues, such as Ralph representing democracy and politics; Jack representing power, evil, and even the devil; Roger representing brutality; and Simon representing a saint or goodness. Interestingly, in a book that presents a struggle between good and evil in human behavior and uses religious symbolism, none of the boys, even in their darkest fear, is heard or described as praying (Oldsey & Weintraub, 1965). In fact, there is no mention of God in the novel.

Ralph, as the protagonist, is most closely associated with the reader, and we may cringe at Ralph's shortcomings. His teasing of Piggy, his fear of the beast, and his lapse into the ritualistic behavior that leads to Simon's murder make him unattractive, but seen against the brutality of Jack or the sadism of Roger, he still gains more reader sympathy than they. Both Ralph and Jack are complicated characters. Jack is described as ugly and violent, and although he is decisive and despotic when he gains control, he also admits to having fears and shows generosity in sharing the fruits of his labor. As Kinkead-Weekes and Gregor (1967) pointed out, Jack is justifiably outraged when Ralph and Piggy condemn him and then expect him to feed them.

As you can see, *Lord of the Flies* provides rich ground for analysis. The book has been given political readings that liken it to Nazi Germany (Crawford, 2002) and psychoanalytical readings that connect it to Freud (Rosenfield, 1961, 1999). Redpath (1986) constructed a structural analysis that traced the alternation between assemblies and trips to the mountain as the defining element in Golding's presentation of the struggle between civilized discourse, as represented by the assemblies, and darkness and fear, as represented by the mountain. Crawford (2002) illustrated that class differences between the boys are significant, with Ralph and Jack both coming from a privileged class and Piggy showing that he is from a less affluent background, which may be yet one more reason—besides his weight, his poor eyesight, and his asthma—that Jack picks on him.

For myself, examining the book in the second decade of the 21st century, *Lord of the Flies* is about how kids treat each other when adults aren't around. The relationships kids develop with each other continue in the presence of adults, but domination through intimidation finds covert means to communicate. Beyond the many layers of symbolism that have been discussed in schools and universities for the past 50 years, *Lord of the Flies* contains a freshness that horrifies because of its treatment of bullying behavior and the message the book sends about the fate of the bullied. Apparently, in the time period when the book was written, bullying was an accepted part of the social structure of British schools (McEwan, qtd. in Crawford, 2002).

I also see an ecological theme emerge from the story that may be a perspective that only has become available in the past 30 years of environmental consciousness. While the island itself has been likened to Eden (Tiger, 1974), a heavenly garden which the boys convert into hell as the darkness within them takes control, I like to consider the book as an ecological fable of how humans attempt to control nature and how, short of being able to control it, they destroy it.

In teaching the novel I can share these pet readings of mine with my students or I can keep them to myself and let the students develop their own readings. One function of this book will be to show you how you can assist students in having their own powerful experience with *Lord of the Flies* without negating your own readings.

The Coral Island

The island setting in *Lord of the Flies* was not created in a vacuum, as Golding was well familiar with the tradition of boys' adventure books that became popular starting in the 19th century and have continued to be popular to the present day, and he mentions several by name, including *The Coral Island*, *Swallows and Amazons*, and *Treasure Island*. Golding acknowledged that the idea for writing *Lord of the Flies* came to him after reading R. M. Ballantyne's *The Coral Island* to his own children and finding it to be an unrealistic representation of how English kids would actually behave in a similar situation of stress. Golding is said to have commented to his wife, Ann, "Wouldn't it be a good idea to write a book about real boys on an island, showing what a mess they'd make?" (Tiger, 1974, p. 38).

In some collected sourcebooks on the novel (see Chapter 8) critics and scholars will include a short synopsis or excerpt from *The Coral Island* and comment that the character names are the same: Jack, Ralph, and Peterkin (who parallels Simon, according to Golding, and has also been linked to Piggy). But a closer look at Ballantyne's book, which is still widely available, reveals the extent to which Golding constructed parallels in his own story. The boys in *The Coral Island* spend a great deal of time exploring their island and thinking about rescue, though not with the desperation of Ralph in *Lord of the Flies*. They also preoccupy themselves with hunting pigs, but where for Golding the violence of the hunt is deeply symbolic, for Ballantyne it is just part of the good fun. Ballantyne's boys kill nearly every animal they encounter, and often with the same level of violence described by Golding:

> Suddenly he leveled his spear, darted forward, and, with a yell that nearly froze the blood in my veins, stabbed the old sow in the heart. Nay, so vigorously was it done that the spear went in at one side and came out at the other!
>
> "Oh Peterkin," said I, going up to him, "what have you done?"
>
> "Done? I've killed their great-great-grandmother, that's all," said he, looking with a somewhat awe-struck expression at the transfixed animal.
>
> "Hallo! what's this?" said Jack, as he came up. "Why Peterkin, you must be fond of a tough chop. If you mean to eat this old hog, she'll try your jaws, I warrant. What possessed you to stick her, Peterkin?"
>
> "Why the fact is, I want a pair of shoes."
>
> "What have your shoes to do with the old hog?" said I, smiling.
>
> "My present shoes have certainly nothing to do with her, " replied Peterkin; "nevertheless, she will have a good deal to do with my future shoes. The fact is, when I saw you floor that pig so neatly, Ralph, it struck me that there was little use in killing another. Then I remembered all at once that I had long wanted some leather or tough substance to make shoes of, and this old grandmother seemed so tough that I just made up my mind to stick her and you see I've done it!"
>
> "That you certainly have, Peterkin," said Jack, as he was examining the transfixed animal. (Ballantyne, 1858, pp. 127–128)

In *The Coral Island*, the boys kill multiple pigs at once and carry them away to be roasted, and they draw a sharp distinction between their noble and fun hunting and the hideous practice of the savage natives, who prefer long pig—i.e., human flesh. When the boys look down from a rock ledge and see a strange and luminous shape in the water of a lagoon on their island, their reaction is to try to kill it with a spear before they determine what it is. They eventually discover that the creature they were trying to kill is nothing more than a trick of light caused by an underwater cave.

At its essence, *The Coral Island* is an adventure story geared toward edification of what we might now consider an imperialistic, Christian, Anglo-centric worldview that celebrates political dominance, dehumanizes indigenous cultures through extreme representation, and treats ecological destruction with nonchalance. Golding's story goes some way toward dismantling that worldview, at least within the context of its own ethos, which is tied to post-World War II reality and a troubling view of human nature.

A reading of *The Coral Island* also shows just how far society has come in its accepted literary treatment of people of color and, particularly, indigenous populations. Ballantyne's adventurers land on their island, never have any conflict with each other, defeat cannibalistic savages and bloodthirsty pirates, and make better everyone they encounter through their British pluck and civilized manners. They echo the imperialist conscience of the White man, as perhaps exemplified by the Kipling poem "The White Man's Burden." For example, the character Peterkin comments early in the book, "We've got an island all to ourselves. We'll take possession in the name of the king; we'll go and enter into the service of its black inhabitants. Of course, we'll rise, naturally, to the top of affairs. White men always do in savage countries" (p. 16).

The narrator, Ralph Rover, often meditates on the savagery in the dark-skinned race, which can only be tamed through conversion to Christianity. Golding refrained, consciously, from inserting any native peoples into *Lord of the Flies*, as he was thus able to depict the descent into savagery of the civilized British schoolchildren without any contrast. A look at Golding's second novel, *The Inheritors*, however, demonstrates Golding's philosophy: that, in encounters between more- and less-advanced societies, the more sophisticated group tends to exhibit the more violent behavior.

Characters in *Lord of the Flies*

Middle and high school students are drawn naturally to character—as they are in the process of defining and developing their own identities—and *Lord of the Flies* offers a number of tantalizing character studies. Here are my thoughts on the major and minor characters of the book, but I encourage you to explore your students' first impressions of the characters and their continued perceptions. For additional summary descriptions of the major characters, see Bloom (2004) and Olsen (2000).

Ralph

Ralph is the first character we meet, described as "The boy with fair hair" (p. 1) in the first words of the novel. Ralph dominates the attention of the narrator throughout the story, though there are notable breaks when the narrator isolates other characters, such as Jack, Simon, and Roger, to describe their singular experiences and psychological tendencies. It is Ralph who stands alone in front of the naval officer at the end of the book, surrounded by the other living boys who ironically accept his leadership by weeping with him, even though seconds before they had been hunting him down with "a stick sharpened at both ends" (p. 221).

Ralph has been described as profoundly average, as an everyman, as the book's moral center, and as a representation of the political (Olsen, 2000). Ralph is distinguished early by his size and strength and by the simple fact that, at Piggy's insistence, he calls the first gathering of the boys by blowing on the found conch shell. He is exuberant and filled with wonder at the luck of his situation, being the first to realize that an island with no grownups could be fun enough to merit standing on one's head. He falls under the influence of Piggy early on, even though he relentlessly teases Piggy, just as the other boys do. Piggy's influence leads Ralph to become preoccupied with keeping a signal fire going to increase the likelihood of rescue, and as the book progresses, that preoccupation leads him to make a series of bad decisions, resulting in the loss of his leadership role—and nearly his life.

Ralph suffers from preadolescent confusion on a number of occasions, especially when in crisis, and other characters become increasingly aware of Ralph's inadequacy as a thinker as the rules set up by the group become more and more onerous. Golding's narrator describes this confusion in a variety of ways, such as Ralph being lost in deep waters, having a flap go down in his brain, or bumping against the limits of his ability to think. For Ralph, however, the urgency of his leadership calls for decision-making skill that outstrips his ability to process the implications of his decisions. When the group reaches a crisis point following the passing of a ship that was missed due to the lack of a signal fire, Ralph calls an assembly to "put things straight" (p. 86). He starts with reasonable demands for drinking water, for sanitary conditions, and for fire, but he complicates the regulations by demanding that no fires be made other than on the mountaintop, and the assembly breaks apart in dissent.

Piggy recognizes Ralph's limitations but also recognizes his glamor and his attractiveness, so Piggy is eager to help Ralph in any way that he can, partly as a way to gain his friendship and partly as a way to save himself from the menace of Jack. Simon recognizes Ralph's leadership and shows support and compassion for him, assuring him in the book's most mystical line that "You'll get back to where you came from" (p. 125). Jack is attracted to Ralph and threatened by him at the same time, and the competition for power between the two boys constitutes a central conflict of the book. As Jack's actions become increasingly savage and cruel, Ralph becomes more sympathetic, but he commits essential moral mistakes, such as continuing to make fun of Piggy (even when he knows Piggy is his greatest ally) and, most grievously, participating in the murder of Simon. By the final chapters of the book, Ralph has lost the ability to lead, and it can be argued that it is Ralph's positioning of Piggy on the rocky cliff that precipitates his death. Following the deaths of Simon and Piggy, Ralph is morally shaken to the core and paralyzed by inaction, which increases Jack's ability to take control of the island. It is only in the final chapter, when he has lost all followers and is being hunted like a pig in the jungle, that he finds singular focus as a savage, attacking when necessary and running away when possible.

Jack

Jack Merridew is described in his first appearance as having a face that is "crumpled and freckled, and ugly without silliness," his eyes "frustrated" and "ready to turn . . . to anger" (p. 17). Much has been said about Jack's transformation from a civilized British "chapter chorister and head boy" (p. 19) to a savage idol, brutally ruling the group of boys through fear and the threat of physical violence. But it is not clear that Jack changes at all during the course of this book. In the first scene he mercilessly leads his choir across the sandy beach with their full-length gowns on in the heat, unwilling to let them break lines regardless of the discomfort they feel, even after a plane crash. He challenges Ralph's authority and never fully accepts his loss in the election for leader. Ralph, perhaps sensing and fearing Jack's malicious nature, awards him the role of head of the military—or in this case, the hunters.

Jack is characterized by his violent bullying of Piggy. He abuses Piggy verbally, punches him in the stomach, and hits him in the head. He steals Piggy's glasses to make fire and resents Ralph for being Piggy's friend, even though Ralph is not really a friend to Piggy. Although it is Roger who ultimately kills Piggy, Roger is in Jack's tribe.

Despite Jack's personality, Ralph finds him to be likable. There is potential that they may become friends, and thus that the island experience may be pleasant. But Jack is also rigid and fearful, which leads to his obsession with the hunt. As he finds success in killing pigs, Jack gains power, especially when compared to Ralph, who can only focus on rescue. Jack becomes physically strong through the exertion of hunting (and a diet that is rich in animal protein), though he is originally described as skinny. Jack's fears are the subject of a central conversation in Chapter 5 of the book, and by recognizing his own fears, he learns how to channel the fear of others for personal gain and power. Following the murder of Simon, which comes about at a time when Jack is in danger of losing his power, Jack uses fear of the beast to bring everyone into line with his regime, and thus becomes a dictator.

A central feature of Jack's transformation, if we consider him changed, is his liberation from conscience through the painting of his face (see Zimbardo, 2007). Wearing a mask turns him into "an awesome stranger" (p. 68), and he becomes "liberated from shame and self-consciousness" (p. 69). Jack discovers and exploits this liberation in building his tribe. He uses rituals of dance, chanting, and feasting to build consensus and group identity. His fateful change is to become a hunter of Ralph, for he cannot harbor any possible challenge to his authority, though there are slight hints in the narrative that Roger may become a threat.

Although Ralph is the protagonist in the novel and Jack is generally considered the antagonist, Jack shows leadership qualities and is drawn well enough by Golding to lead us to consider that he may have been a positive influence on the island if the boys had organized themselves more intelligently. Jack cannot be blamed for going off on his own in the face of Ralph's scolding over the fire, but he can be blamed for his vicious bullying of Piggy and his violent, authoritarian rule, which ultimately leads him to become a sociopath.

Piggy

The fact that we never learn this child's name is a great trick of the author's, as we are forced to call him by the nickname he hates in our discussions of the book. He is described in the first scene in complete contrast to Ralph, and he does most of the talking. He annoys Ralph and, vicariously, the reader through his incessant talking and whining. Although all of the characters in this book are tragic, Piggy may be the most so, as he is the ultimate outsider. Even Simon, who is sacrificed at the hands of the group, is well liked, despite his otherness. Piggy is the object of derision, violence, teasing, and ostracism. No one befriends him, except perhaps Simon, who shows compassion for him, even though Piggy rejects Simon as "batty" (p. 181).

Piggy is capable of hatred, as he hates Jack and fears him. His relationship with Jack forms a complementary conflict in the narrative, and for some students who read this work, Piggy's victimization through Jack's bullying will dominate their experience with the text. Despite our attempts to focus student attention on political aspects of the novel or power struggles between Ralph and Jack, for a student who is the victim of bullying in life and at school, Piggy's story will resonate above all others. Piggy is different. Piggy is bullied. Piggy is killed. End of story. As teachers, we need to be aware of how directly and accurately Golding depicts physical and verbal domination.

Another dominant feature of Piggy's is his practical realism. He doesn't believe in the beast and he believes in the rational man. He is the voice of logic and has been described as the symbol of reason in counterpoint to Simon's mysticism. Ralph realizes that Piggy can think and that his thinking is necessary for the success of the society the boys are building on the island, but Ralph can't make himself actually like Piggy. Piggy cannot do physical labor on account of his asthma (ass-mar, as Ralph calls it), he doesn't seem to like doing any work at all, and he is unable to organize the littluns. Ralph resents Piggy's assistance when he has trouble thinking.

Piggy's other physical limitation is his poor eyesight, which becomes an issue when the group realizes that his glasses are needed to start fire. This community need could make Piggy a valuable member of the society; instead, it only serves to alienate him further, as Jack's tribe realizes that the glasses may be used without the owner. Jack first breaks Piggy's glasses when he hits Piggy on the head, and later steals the glasses outright.

The last image of Piggy is as a twitching body lying on a rock with his brains pouring out. But Piggy's symbolic presence continues to be felt after his death, haunting Ralph and appearing on the penultimate page of the novel, when Jack is described as a "little boy who wore the remains of an extraordinary black cap on his red hair and who carried the remains of a pair of spectacles at his waist" (p. 234). It is Piggy for whom Ralph weeps at the end of the book, where he is described as a "true, wise friend" (p. 235). In a sociological reading of the novel, this line may serve as a revelation, with Piggy finally earning Ralph's friendship only through death.

Simon

Simon is in many ways the most unconventional character in the book. He first appears as a boy who often faints (as Jack indicates in Chapter 1), and he later has a fit that involves a burst blood vessel in his nose. He becomes paralyzed by anxiety when speaking to the group; consequently, his actions speak louder than his words.

Simon was the most difficult character for Golding to write (Carey, 2009). Golding's original manuscript identified Simon as mystical and in direct communication with a deity, but Golding's editor, Edward Monteith, helped him tone Simon down to the point where he passes as an actual kid, like the others in his foibles but unlike the others in his charity and courage. Simon is one of my favorite characters in literature, and he saves this novel from the utter darkness under which the other characters fall. His death appears more inevitable than tragic, but it is the turning point in the novel. His deeds exemplify the best in humanity and the best we can hope for in our own children (and ourselves).

Throughout the novel, Simon partakes in a series of charitable acts: He likes all the other characters, including Jack; he offers Piggy meat when Jack rejects him; and he assures Ralph, in his hour of need, that he will get back home. He discovers the true nature of the beast on the hill. He determines to tell the others the truth.

He dies for his knowledge because he doesn't remember his own warnings that the beast may be "only us" (p. 98).

According to Delbaere-Garant (1978) and others, Simon is the connection to the natural world, and his death rips the group loose from their own connection to the balance of nature. Simon can be seen as opposite to Piggy in the nature versus science or spirit versus reason dichotomies, and he may be seen as opposite to Roger in the love versus hate dichotomy.

Simon's interview with the Lord of the Flies (a pig's head on a stick) is the most challenging and interpretive scene in the book. It is the voice of the Lord of the Flies that convinces Simon to climb the mountain to confront the beast; he resolves to go forward, saying, "What else is there to do?" (p. 167). Following his ascent up the mountain and his realization that the beast is just a dead man, Simon rushes down to tell the others and is brutally murdered. The detailed and beautiful transformation of Simon's body by the phosphorescent sea animals in the tide and the description of the sea carrying him away reinforce the symbol of his connection with nature. Simon's death scene is particularly well directed in Peter Brook's 1963 film, with Simon's body slowly turning over in the water with light glittering around it and the beautiful (and ironic) voices of a boys' choir singing over. As Baker (1963) commented, Simon is doomed because "In whatever culture he appears, the saint is doomed by his insights" (p. 28).

Samneric

Sam and Eric, two energetic and somewhat facile twins, help to fill out the cast of this island tragedy. They represent regular kids who forget their responsibilities, though not maliciously, and who seem conscientious in the way that most kids are conscientious: that is, as long as it doesn't conflict with more interesting pursuits. They remain faithful to Ralph's leadership longer than anyone but Piggy and physically fight the intruders who come to steal Piggy's glasses (though somewhat comically, as after the skirmish it seems that Eric fought Ralph by mistake). They are eventually tortured by Roger and turned into unwilling participants in the hunt for Ralph.

It is difficult to blame Samneric (as they are often called) for their behavior, even though they commit key mistakes that figure into the novel's outcome. Golding's narrator implies that it is Samneric who leave the signal fire unattended at the critical time, when the ship passes. It is Samneric who first see the dead parachutist and identify it as the beast, rather than question their own perceptions of what they saw in the dawn's early light. It is also Samneric who initiate the denial of participation in Simon's murder, a lead that Piggy and Ralph all too willingly follow. Students may explore why Samneric are portrayed as a unit, and what that says about the boys' tendency to want to reduce each other to comprehensible types. As it is easiest to think of Simon as batty and Piggy as an outsider, it is easiest to think of Sam and Eric as one person (Samneric) and thus perhaps as interchangeable common men.

Roger

Roger has been called the foil to Simon, or vice versa (Olsen, 2000), and he is generally associated with darkness and evil. He is first referred to as "a slight, furtive boy whom no one knew, who kept to himself with an inner intensity of avoidance and secrecy" (p. 19). He is called "the dark boy" (p.19), but it is he who first calls for a vote for chief.

One of the most compelling scenes in the book portrays Roger throwing rocks at the littlun Henry—throwing to miss, but feeling exhilaration in the act, as though he is already realizing a tendency toward violence for pleasure's sake. In this scene, society's taboos against unreasoned violence are already fading in Roger, foreshadowing greater violence to come.

It is Roger who kills Piggy and who tortures Samneric, the "hangman's horror" (p. 210) clinging to him, and there are implications that Jack himself may not be able to contain Roger's sadism. Roger doesn't need Jack's orders to sharpen a stick at both ends before the hunt for Ralph.

Maurice, Robert, Bill, and Other Biguns

Golding creates the illusion of a larger group by picking out certain boys to give names and minor but differentiated roles, with the implication that there are similar others. It is unclear exactly which of the boys was in the original choir, but three who are given certain characteristics and enough distinct personality to become real for us are Maurice, Robert, and Bill. Maurice is the second biggest boy in the choir (behind Jack), and he is described by Ralph as a "practiced debater" (p. 86). Both he and Robert stand in as pigs when the boys play at killing. The two, along with Simon, are described as inhabiting a "dubious region" (p. 63) between biguns and littluns (which seems to contradict the earlier description of Maurice as next in size to Jack). Robert, whose name is close to "Roger," is the one who demonstrates to Roger the operation of the lever. Bill appears from the narrative to be one of the last boys to defect from Ralph's tribe to Jack's. Again, none of these characters as individuals affect the course of the action, but as a group they make possible Jack's rise to power, and by having names and hints of personality, they remind us of the boys' general descent into savagery.

Johnny, the Boy With the Mulberry-Colored Birthmark, Phil, Percival, Henry, and Other Littluns

As with the biguns, Golding gives the impression of a large group of boys by referring to littluns periodically throughout the book, naming a few of them and giving them distinct personality traits, and then narrating a few pivotal scenes that cast littluns into leading roles. They are largely ignored by the biguns, but, ironically, they have a deep influence over the group through their fears and their insistence on different occasions that a beast exists.

The littluns are left unattended mostly because the biguns lack paternal consciousness, with the exception of Simon, who feeds the littluns by handing them fruit they cannot reach. Piggy is unable to even count them, and the other boys never make the effort. While Piggy appears to care about them by advocating for them and speaking for them at assemblies, even he loses interest in them as the book progresses. They are described as living an "intense life of their own" (p. 63), having chronic diarrhea and crying at night in their collective and individual fears.

The first littlun we meet is Johnny, who appears energetic and playful. The next littlun in the spotlight is the boy with the mulberry-colored birthmark on his face, who disappears after the first fire gets out of the boys' control and is assumed to have died in the fire. This first disappearance signals not just the possibility of death happening on the island, but the possibility that death could come at the boys' own hands or by their own agency. In the first fire and, perhaps most importantly, in the final fire in the book, Golding offers us no way of knowing how many littluns may have perished.

The littluns who are named fulfill different roles. Phil holds the group in fascinated captivation as he tells of his dream, struggling with "twisty things in the trees" (p. 93). Percival Wemys Madison spends most of his time crying. He, like the other boys, is filthy, and he insists that the beast is real. He is bullied by the biguns and by his peers. He likes to recite his name, address, and telephone number, but by the end of the book he can remember none of these, symbolizing the regression of the tribe. Johnny, who is "well built, with fair hair and a natural belligerence" (p. 64), observes Maurice and Roger kicking sand into Percival's face and imitates the gesture, which makes Percival cry. Henry, who is more athletic and vital than Percival, becomes a full-fledged member of Jack's tribe, serving as a reminder that the boys think they are playing; Henry cannot know the moral implications of his identity as one of Jack's henchmen.

Three other boys in the book who are given names are Wilfred, Stanley, and Harold. It is unclear whether they are biguns or littluns. Wilfred is tied up to be beaten for no apparent reason, and Stanley starts to remind Jack that the boys had killed the beast on the beach, which Jack refutes. Harold's name appears only in the initial roll call.

The Beast

The beast is a character in the book because the boys believe it is a character, not because it exists. It begins as a "snake-thing" (p. 35) in the mind of the ill-fated littlun with the mulberry-colored birthmark. It evolves into something that wanders about at night, and then is given a misinterpreted flesh and blood manifestation in the dead parachutist. As the parachutist is the "sign" (p. 105) from the adult world that Ralph had wished for in the chapter previous to its appearance, it marks the first representative of adults and demonstrates the adult preoccupation with war. It is thus fitting that the parachutist assumes the role of beast in the boys' misperceptions. Through Jack's vivid imagination, the beast becomes a sort of god that must be propitiated by sacrifice. The beast then briefly and tragically takes the form of Simon during the frenzy of the storm dance. Following the death of Simon, the beast both circumscribes Jack's power and creates his power, as Jack knows how to channel fear of the beast into power of his own. Jack and Roger and the rest of the boys become the beast they fear, just as Simon had predicted.

The Lord of the Flies

The Lord of the Flies is an imagined speaker during the interview scene with Simon in Chapter 8. The head of the killed sow that is placed on a long stick and left to appease the beast becomes the voice of what Simon fears is happening to the group of boys. The phrase "Lord of the Flies" refers to Beelzebub, an indirect reference to the devil (Epstein, 1997). The dialogue between the Lord of the Flies and Simon comes as close as possible to directly stating the problem of the novel: that the growing evil is within the boys themselves. Simon both creates the voice and recognizes its unreality, but the intensity of knowing what the Lord of the Flies tells him leads Simon to faint and causes a blood vessel to burst in his nose.

The Naval Captain

The second representative of the adult world, this gentleman "rescues" the boys at the novel's end—but by then rescue is pointless, as it is too late to save Piggy and Simon, and it is too late to save the rest of the boys from their own natures. The Captain's authority, his perception of Ralph's physical state and truthfulness, and his self-righteous admonition of the boys force us to shift our perspective away from the horrifying story we have witnessed and see, as though from a distance, a group of dirty, ragged little castaways.

The Island

The role of the island itself is almost akin to a character role, so dominant and pivotal is the natural world in the story. The boys' relationship with the island is filled with antithesis. The island is nurturer and torturer to the boys. It is killer and victim, a place of freedom and a place of imprisonment. The nighttime island is full of noises and unspoken terrors. The island also contains a fun swimming pool, an abundance of food, and pigs to hunt. The boys get injured by trying to run through the jungle. They get caught up in the creepers, they hang on to the ledges, and they get burned by the hot sun shining down on the sand. Golding spends so much time painstakingly describing individual features of the island that the sheer volume of features becomes overwhelming. By the end of the book, the boys transform the island into an inferno.

Plot Summary

This plot summary is just a scratch, for quick reference. For a full, scene-by-scene reading, see Chapter 4.

Chapter 1

The first two characters introduced, Ralph and Piggy, encounter each other in a "scar" (p. 1) smashed into a tropical island by the wreckage of their airplane. Ralph shows little interest in Piggy until they find a conch shell half buried in a lagoon. Piggy teaches Ralph to blow the conch, and when he does, other boys gather on the platform where Ralph and Piggy are. Children between the ages of 6 and 12 appear alone and in groups, including a choir that is led by a tall, severe boy named Jack. One choir member, a boy named Simon, faints in the heat. After some dialogue, the boys understand that there are no adults on the island, and they vote to have Ralph be their chief, which upsets Jack. Ralph puts Jack in charge of the choir, and Jack designates them as hunters. Piggy is insulted by Jack and teased by the entire group. Ralph, Jack, and Simon leave the others and explore the island.

Chapter 2

The boys hold a second assembly so that Ralph, Jack, and Simon can report what they saw on the island. The boys discuss rules they shall have, and they designate the conch as the object indicating who can speak. A little boy with a mulberry-colored birthmark suggests that he has seen a "snake-thing" or "beastie" (p. 35) in the night, and the boys debate its existence. Ralph proposes keeping a signal fire to increase chances of rescue, and the boys all run off to the mountain to start a fire, leaving Piggy disgusted by their childish behavior. The group gathers firewood, and Jack forcefully takes Piggy's glasses to light it. Piggy scolds the group and then notices that their fire has gotten out of control. The fire burns a section of the mountain, and Piggy shouts out that the boy with the mulberry-colored birthmark is missing.

Chapter 3

Jack is shown in the intensity and diligence of the hunt. After another close miss trying to kill a pig, he returns to the beach, where Ralph and Simon are working on shelters. The boys talk about how no one is helping, and tension rises between Ralph and Jack over division of responsibilities. Ralph and Jack head down the beach to check on the signal fire and find it is going, but they argue over the need for meat versus the need for shelters. Simon is shown entering the forest, with littluns following him. Simon feeds the littluns with fruit that they cannot reach themselves, and then retreats to a secret bower in the jungle.

Chapter 4

Time has passed and the boys have established certain routines. Three littluns play on the beach and two bigger boys, Maurice and Roger, walk through their area, destroying their sand castles. A littlun named Percival cries and another littlun, Johnny, throws sand in his face. The third littlun, Henry, walks down the beach, where Roger stands behind a coconut tree and throws rocks at him, aiming to miss. Jack, meanwhile, discovers that he can camouflage himself by painting different colors of mud on his face. He finds Roger and recruits other boys, including Samneric, to go hunting. Back at the site of the shelters, Ralph demonstrates a benign intolerance of Piggy. Ralph then spots a ship on the horizon, and the boys run up the mountain, discovering that the signal fire has gone out. Jack and his gang of hunters come to the fire spot with their first killed pig. Ralph and Jack argue, and Piggy steps in, only to be hit in the stomach and head by Jack, which breaks Piggy's glasses. The boys then cook the pig and eat it, chanting, "Kill the pig. Cut her throat. Bash her in" (p. 82). The chapter ends with Ralph calling for an assembly.

Chapter 5

This chapter opens with a description of Ralph's internal monologue as he prepares to say what he must at the assembly. His sense of his own limitations is explored, and he recognizes that "Piggy could think" (p. 85). At the assembly, Ralph gives a speech where he lays out rules regarding the fire and other matters, such as water supply and sanitation. He then opens discussion of the boys' fear and the assembly becomes disorderly. Jack asserts himself and reinforces the boys' fear by mentioning an "animal" (p. 91), even while claiming that there is no beast. Piggy speaks and is again teased by all. Piggy brings forth the littlun Percival, who speaks of a beastie. Simon admits that he has been walking around at night, which may have scared the littluns, but then a debate about ghosts erupts. Simon says that maybe there is a beast, but that it might just be the boys themselves. Ralph and Jack argue, and the assembly breaks apart when Jack claims he will "beat and beat and beat" the beast if it is real (p. 101). As the other boys scatter, Ralph, Simon, and Piggy are left feeling helpless and wishing for a sign from the adult world.

Chapter 6

An air battle takes place above the island, and a dead parachutist falls, his lines becoming entangled in the trees at the top of the mountain. Samneric are on duty at the signal fire the next morning, and they catch sight of the parachutist. They mistake it for the beast and run down the mountain to tell the others. The boys discuss what should be done, and they decide to look for the beast, figuring the rock formations at the island's end are the logical place for the beast to live. Jack challenges the use of the conch in the meeting. On the way to the end of the island, Simon tells Ralph that he does not believe in the beast. The boys go to what is referred to as the Castle Rock, where they find no beast but find instead the makings of a good fort and large, balancing boulders that may be dislodged and sent tumbling down through the trees or to the ocean. Ralph insists that the boys go on to the mountain to restart a signal fire, and the other boys reluctantly obey.

Chapter 7

This chapter starts with a description of Ralph's physical and mental state. He is clearly stressed and very filthy. The boys continue their search for the beast and head up the mountain. On the way, they encounter a boar, and Ralph wounds it. Jack is wounded and a struggle over their stature in the eyes of the other boys ensues. The climb up the mountain is extremely difficult given the route they have chosen, and the boys want to go back to the beach, but Ralph, sensing a challenge from Jack, decides to go on, with just Jack and Roger accompanying him. In the fading light of dusk, the boys see the dead parachutist but mistake it as the beast and run all the way back to the shelters.

Chapter 8

There is an assembly to discuss the beast. Jack tells the boys that Ralph has insulted the hunters and calls for a second vote for chief. When he loses the vote,

Jack departs in angry tears, saying he's "not going to play any longer" (p. 145). The others decide to build a fire on the beach, but while gathering wood, Ralph notices that most of the other boys have left to go follow Jack. Simon retreats to his secret place, where he witnesses Jack and the hunters killing a large sow. The boys leave the sow's head stuck on the end of a stick lodged in the rock to appease the beast. Simon approaches the pig's head and sees the flies gathering on a pile of guts. Jack's group attacks Ralph and Piggy; they take a burning branch for their fire, and then invite Ralph and the others to a feast of pig. Ralph calls an assembly with the remaining boys to discuss their situation as a thunderstorm builds in the background. The chapter ends with Simon having a hallucinatory conversation with the "Lord of the Flies" (p. 163), as represented by the pig's head. The Lord of the Flies tells Simon that the others are going to "do you" (p. 165). Simon faints and the chapter ends.

Chapter 9

A storm has been building on the island, and darkness is coming. Simon awakens from his faint and leaves the site of the pig's head to climb the mountain. He discovers the dead parachutist, frees it from the tangle, and runs to tell the other boys. At the platform, Ralph and Piggy consider their options and decide to head to Jack's feast. Awkwardness rules at the feast as Ralph challenges Jack and reminds the boys that they have no shelters. As the thunderstorm hits, Jack leads the boys in a violent dance. Simon comes running out of the jungle, and, mistaking him for the beast, the boys murder him on the beach. The dead parachutist is blown over the boys and out to sea, and Simon's body is embraced by the luminous creatures in the tide and carried away by the water.

Chapter 10

Ralph and Piggy discover one another in the dawn and argue about what happened at the fire. Samneric join them, and they argue about keeping a fire. Samneric hint that they were not involved in Simon's death. Jack moves his tribe to the Castle Rock, where Robert shows Roger how he has rigged a lever under a balancing rock. As Ralph, Piggy, and Samneric try to sleep, Jack and two others attack and steal Piggy's glasses, leaving Piggy sightless and Ralph badly beaten.

Chapter 11

Ralph, Piggy, and Samneric have a small assembly to decide what to do, and Piggy resolves to go to the Castle Rock to ask for his glasses. Ralph doesn't think it is a good idea but agrees that they all should go. When they get there, Ralph and Jack argue over everything that has happened while Roger throws small rocks from above. Jack and Ralph fight briefly; then Jack has his hunters grab Samneric and tie them down. As Jack's tribe prepares to attack Ralph, Piggy, holding the conch, scolds the group for acting like kids. Roger pushes the lever on the big rock and sends it tumbling down, shattering the conch and knocking Piggy off the cliff and 40 feet down to his death. Ralph flees as the other boys throw spears at him.

Chapter 12

Ralph tries to decide what to do in his desperation. He wanders the island and then returns to the Castle Rock. He sees Samneric on guard and learns from them that the group will hunt Ralph in the morning. Ralph learns that Roger has sharpened a stick at both ends, presumably to behead Ralph and stick his head on it. The boys hunt Ralph, and when they find him but cannot get to him, they roll rocks down a hill to smash him. When that doesn't work, they start a fire close to where Ralph is hiding. As the island goes up in flames, Ralph is flushed out and fights his way down to the beach, where he falls and rolls over, expecting to be killed. He looks up and sees a naval officer, who has come to rescue them. As the officer questions Ralph, he and the other boys begin to weep.

Once you have oriented yourself to the novel and its author, it is time to consider ways to prepare your students for the literary journey. Chapter 3 will provide a number of prereading activities to increase student interest and prepare the soil for their intellectual engagement with the text.

"It's like in a book": Prereading Activities for *Lord of the Flies*

Preparing students to read *Lord of the Flies* may involve simply handing out the texts and inviting them to open to page 1, or it may involve a series of anticipatory activities to orient them to the coming experience or to the goals of the unit. My own preference is to avoid material that includes an interpretation of the text, as that will negatively affect your students' ability to construct their own initial reading of the text. I prefer for them to approach the text with a relatively naïve stance, certainly bringing to bear their previous knowledge and reading experiences, but not influenced by CliffsNotes analyses or even the teacher's biases. Secondary sources can and should come into play during postreading study, when taking a second or third (or fourth or fifth) look at the text becomes essential.

I do not find extensive historical contextualizing or attention to the author's biography necessary as a precondition to reading, but I also do not see any harm in these pursuits. Students can learn about the author as their interest in the work grows, and they can learn about the historical context of the novel in the process of making sense of the world portrayed in its pages. In the case of *Lord of the Flies*, historical context and author biography are at once vitally important and irrelevant, depending upon one's approach to interpretation. Information on Golding's life and his own recorded explanations of the personal experiences that gave rise to the story are readily available, and yet the story itself attempts (almost successfully) to avoid *all* references to a specific time period, so as to mythologize the events.

While having students imagine themselves stranded on a tropical island can be a good prereading activity, I have seen teachers who direct students to pretend they are stranded on an island and to generate a list of survival supplies or essential tools, a concern that doesn't come into play in *Lord of the Flies*, as the boys have plenty of food and fresh water available to them and the capacity to make fire and build shelters. A more productive use of such visualization would be to have students imagine what interpersonal skills they would need to survive being stranded with fellow human beings. It is also important to note that this book is rarely read in school with children who are the age equivalent of the characters, so it is an abstract exercise for them to cast themselves in the same situation. Related to this concern, you might ask your students to visit a 5th or 6th grade school playground and spend time observing how kids interact with one another, how they negotiate rules of play, and generally how cruelly or kindly they treat one another. If you are reading the story with 12-year-olds, then you can use your students as authorities on behavior.

What I present here is a series of prereading activities that are easy to complete in a short period of time in your classroom and that should, if well implemented, stimulate student interest to read and to think about the book's central concerns. You may use one of them, a few of them, or all of them, depending on the time you have budgeted in your schedule. I am not suggesting that you draw out the number of weeks you spend studying the novel (see Chapter 2 for discussion of unit design), and especially not that you spend more than 2 or 3 days preparing students to read before diving into the book itself. Remember that students will eventually fend for themselves in their encounters with literature, and we want to foster the independent reading habits that will serve them well in college and adult life. That being said, here are a few options.

ACTIVITY (SAS #1): YOU UNDER PRESSURE

Have students imagine themselves in the most stressful situations they have experienced thus far in their lives. Using journal writing, have the students try to recall how their behavior changed or was affected by the stress of that situation. Have them describe examples of things they did or said that, upon reflection, were not what they would ordinarily do or say when not under pressure. In particular, have them write about how the stress affected their interaction with others. For students who have experienced personal trauma or loss, this may prove to be a difficult or emotional activity, but thinking about it and sharing in small groups and/or with the entire class will orient them to the situation the boys in the novel face. When situations in the book arise that demonstrate what we would consider extreme, unusual, and perhaps unsanctioned behavior in the boys, you can recall this prereading exercise and ask students to discuss how the stress of the situation may be affecting individual characters.

These Are Our Rules

This is a common prereading activity for *Lord of the Flies*, as it imitates exactly the situation the boys face in the opening chapter of the novel. If done well, it can get your students thinking about their own agency in determining the code of their behavior, their individual positions in society, and their responsibilities toward one other. How complex you make this activity depends upon the time you have and other factors, such as your unit goals. If you are reading *Lord of the Flies* as part of a larger unit on societal organization, government, or the nature of power, you may want to spend some time on this and employ a mock legislative process, with committees, introduction of bills, and so forth. If, on the other hand, you simply want students to think briefly about the rules they would prefer to live by if granted the freedom to make those rules, the activity can be done in the space of 20–30 minutes.

ACTIVITY (SAS #2): THESE ARE OUR RULES

Give students a free-writing prompt such as the following: "The members of this class are going to create a society for themselves. As part of your charter, you have the freedom to set rules for yourselves. These rules will govern every aspect of your lives, from work to play to getting food and living arrangements. Generate a list of rules that you would like your community to follow, then prioritize that list from most important (1) to least important (10)."

After students have generated their individual lists, have them assemble into small groups and compare notes, discussing the lists with each other. Ask them to come to consensus on 3–5 rules that they would adopt.

With each group representing their part of the class community, have them come together as a class and choose one classmate to be leader. This alone may prove difficult, but once they have chosen that leader, it is the leader's job to listen to the rules proposed by the small groups and decide which rules the community will adopt. The leader may decide to adopt the rules by him or herself, or the leader may let the community vote for the rules.

Assuming your class is able to succeed in the previous steps and adopt a set of rules to govern themselves, then discuss (either in small groups or as a class) what the penalties will be for violation of each rule that was adopted. They may also discuss how those penalties will be enforced, or whether they can be enforced without threat of violence.

Finally, have the class reflect on the activity and what difficulties they faced. Share your own observations of how the individuals cooperated or competed for power in the conversation.

During the process of reading *Lord of the Flies*, you may return to this activity to remind students of what challenges they faced, and also to remind them that the characters in the novel are ages 6–12, with no one older present.

Problem Situations

This activity can be done in 15–20 minutes from start to finish, and it works well to orient your students to the complex situations characters face in the novel. The goal is to get them thinking about their own decision making when faced with certain dilemmas. Separate students into groups of three or four and distribute the following scenarios, one to each group, so that all groups have different scenarios and all scenarios are represented. If you have a small class, you may either have them work in pairs or choose scenarios to leave out. You may also choose one of the scenarios to consider as a whole class to introduce the activity and model the process of thinking.

ACTIVITY (SAS #3): PROBLEM SITUATIONS

Distribute one of the following scenarios to each group, and have them generate possible responses to the questions asked. Once all groups have generated responses, discuss them as a class.

1. You discover that something a group of friends believes to be true, something that has caused conflict among them, is actually false. You want to share the new information with them, knowing that they may not believe you right away. Your friends are gathered at a party. Do you go straight to the party and tell all of them at once or do you wait and tell them individually?

2. You know someone who thinks of you as a friend, and you have spent time with him, although you find him annoying at times. He has made several attempts to be your friend, and you have been nice at times and not nice at other times. You witness another potential friend calling him names and punching him in the stomach. No adult is there to intervene. What are your options? What do you do?

3. You are in a setting with some kids your age and some younger kids, but no adults are present. You and the older kids are not paying attention to the younger kids, but you happen to notice that the younger kids are doing something that could be dangerous and cause them harm. What are your options? What do you do?

4. You are at a job, and the boss is not present. It is clear to you that not everyone is pulling his or her weight at work, and you are frustrated because it is causing more work for you, and you are already behind on your own work. What are your options? What do you do?

5. You have a job to do that is important to you and to your community. Everyone relies on you to do this job, but your friends are urging you to leave the job for a while and come with them to do something fun. You know your responsibility, but you also don't want to jeopardize your friendships. How do you decide what to do? Do you leave the job or say no to your friends?

6. You believe that a friend is too superstitious and is afraid of things you don't believe in, such as ghosts. You see that the person's fear is affecting his or her behavior. What are your options? What do you do?

7. You find that, due to a lack of judgment, you and your friends have done something that caused serious harm to another person. You believe that what you've done is wrong and you feel guilty for it. Some of your friends are making excuses and pretending that nothing happened. What are your options? What do you do?

One nice feature of the Problem Situations activity is that it gives students the opportunity to think about and consider difficult situations in a nonthreatening and supportive atmosphere. Knowing that these situations are hypothetical allows them to cast themselves in the role without being self-conscious. The other and more salient benefit of the activity is that it previews for students situations that will arise in the text. The activity thus serves as a comprehension aid, as students will be familiar with dilemmas when they encounter them in the text, and they will be interested to see how the characters deal with those situations as compared to how they themselves would have acted.

Theme Tableau

This activity has many variations and applications across the curriculum. A 3-dimensional "tableau vivant"—French for "living picture"—gives students something to visually observe and allows them to study what is communicated by positions and expressions of characters relative to one another, as though studying museum pieces. The function of doing this activity as a prereading exercise is to introduce students to themes in the book by engaging them physically and visually in the images suggested by those themes. A tableau also serves to create class community and cooperation and to develop performance skills in a nonthreatening environment.

It is wise to only do two or three of these with one group of students before switching and having a different group come to the front. It is also important to have the group take their positions in a part of the classroom where you and other students may walk around them to see different perspectives. I would not suggest that you do every one of the prompt words listed below, but that you use the activity to get students thinking about how what we experience mentally and emotionally may be manifested physically. Follow the tableau activity with reflective journal writing. I will return to a short discussion of this activity in Chapter 5, as a performance option following the initial reading of the text.

ACTIVITY: THEME TABLEAU

Bring to the front of the class five or six student volunteers, mixed male and female, and tell them to bunch up in a huddle. Tell them you are going to give them a word prompt, and they will have 5 seconds to strike a pose and then freeze. Before they freeze, they must be in physical contact with at least one other member of the group. The goal is for the group to communicate the prompt word through the positions the members of the group take. Ask them to keep in mind that they can make use of different levels, as in lying down, kneeling, or climbing on one another. After the group freezes, the rest of the students will study the tableau and comment on what is communicated, treating the group as though they are a sculpture in a museum. Possible prompt words for *Lord of the Flies* tableaux include:

- Warm-up Tableau: Celebration

- Tableau 1: Confusion

- Tableau 2: Order

- Tableau 3: Fear

- Tableau 4: Power

- Tableau 5: War

- Tableau 6: Survival

- Tableau 7: Rescue

Protector/Aggressor

Another activity that fits well with *Lord of the Flies* is a game called Protector-Aggressor. It is adapted from Augusto Boal's (2002) *Games for Actors and Non-Actors.*

Follow up this activity with a discussion of how we develop protective relationships with others and how we perceive threats to our safety. This can be a powerful conversation, especially for students in urban environments who feel very real threats to their security in their own neighborhoods. As students reflect on their own sense of security and connection to others, they will gain a heightened awareness of the issues of safety experienced by the characters in the book.

Chapters 5–7 will further develop opportunities for discussion, writing, and project work related to the themes of safety and community.

ACTIVITY: PROTECTOR/AGGRESSOR

To play "Protector-Aggressor" with your students, you will need to move all of the desks to the periphery of your room or find another space that is large enough for all of the students to have room to walk around freely. Have students walk in random paths, silently, imagining that they are part of a community. You can give students various prompts to express communal sentiments, to be expressed only through gestures, movement, and facial expression, such as "tragedy," "springtime," and "prosperity." Then, as they continue to walk around the space you have created, say to them: "One of the other people in this town is your protector. That person cannot know that you have chosen him or her to be your protector. Just silently choose someone and keep them in your mind as you move about the town." Give students a few seconds to silently choose their protector. Then say, "Okay, I assume that everyone has chosen a protector. Now, you must identify, silently and only to yourself, another person in this group who is your aggressor. That person cannot know he or she is your aggressor—just keep it in your mind. So now you have a protector in the crowd and an aggressor, someone who is out to get you." Give students a few seconds to make sure they have chosen an aggressor. Continue with, "Now your goal, without talking or grabbing, is to keep your protector between you and your aggressor. Go."

What typically ensues is a little like mayhem, as some students will have picked for their aggressor the very person who chose them for protector. The playing space becomes twisted as people chase one another and rotate and spin to try to get away from their aggressors. Call "stop" or "freeze" whenever appropriate and debrief with students regarding what is happening in the scene. The activity can be connected to the story, wherein relationships are complicated, and the boys on the island form alliances for protection, only to see those alliances twisted or broken. The other benefit of this game, besides the fact that it is fun to play, is that you get students physically involved in the abstract ideas represented in the text. When students are reading *Lord of the Flies*, they may refer to the game in terms of defining relationships, such as, "Jack is Piggy's aggressor, and Piggy believes that Ralph is his protector, but Ralph isn't ready for that role."

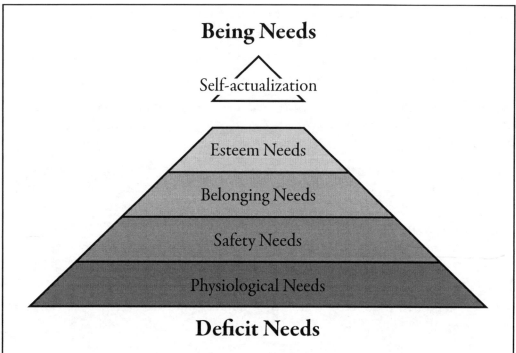

Figure 1. Maslow's Hierarchy of Needs. *Note.* Adapted from "Abraham Maslow" by C. G. Boeree, 2006.

Maslow's Hierarchy of Needs

A good follow-up to the Protector-Aggressor activity and the tableau is to introduce students to Maslow's hierarchy of needs. This is a great way to educate them on theory related to the deeply personal and emotional themes developed in the novel. Understanding the hierarchy will give students an additional frame of reference for discussion of individual character motivations during various stages of the text. Several different descriptions of Maslow's theory are easily accessible on the web, but I find Boeree's (2006) analysis to be accessible for students, with effective graphics. You may find it at http://webspace.ship.edu/cgboer/maslow.html. A basic visual representation of Maslow's hierarchy, as taken from the website, can be found in Figure 1.

How much time you spend examining Maslow's hierarchy is dependent on how central you wish to make it in your approach to the novel. It can serve as an organizing principle for discussion and analysis of the novel, or it can reinforce other perspectives. One of the project ideas in Chapter 7 involves a deeper development of the hierarchy in relation to the experiences of the characters in *Lord of the Flies*. As with the Problem Situations activity above, you can have your students examine model scenarios of conflict and ask them to identify the levels on the hierarchy that dominate those situations.

ACTIVITY (SAS #4): GOOD LEADERSHIP— WHAT DOES IT LOOK LIKE?

Have students brainstorm qualities they like to see in leaders. Students can search online for quotes or short readings related to leadership, or they can ask their parents and other adults what they value in leaders. Have the class compile a list mounted to the wall.

Movie Trailer

The Movie Trailer activity (see pages 45–46) can be done in 10–15 minutes in your classroom and is designed to create interest and enthusiasm for the coming reading. Assign roles to the readers in your class who will use loud and effective voices. All students who don't have speaking roles will fill the roles of "All" and "Sound Effects" in the script. Have students stand in a circle to read the Movie Trailer script. It is important for you as the teacher to take the role of narrator, to keep the piece moving and to provide emotion. The reading should move quickly and take only about 2–3 minutes from start to finish. When students have completed the staged reading, have them comment on what they think the book is going to be about based on the trailer.

After students have read and studied *Lord of the Flies*, you may have a small group of students who want to return to the Movie Trailer and produce their own with video images and sound effects.

Descriptive Writing

Another prereading activity is to have students complete a descriptive writing exercise (see page 38). This will get students to start thinking about author's craft (Common Core) and to appreciate the work involved in painting a realistic narrative scene. The activity will also give students practice in descriptive writing from sensory experience.

When students read the opening pages of the *Lord of the Flies*, have them compare Golding's technique in describing the island, the meeting of Ralph and Piggy, and the finding of the conch with their own experience constructing a scene with a symbolic, or at least useful, object.

ACTIVITY (SAS #5): DESCRIPTIVE WRITING EXERCISE

Ask students to find a natural setting, an outdoor space, and try to describe everything they see there in as much detail as possible. You can either do this as a class activity, leading your students to an outdoor space, or, better yet, assign this first step as homework, so as to elicit a variety of settings. Ask them to immerse themselves in the plants, the animals, the insects, and the other objects or structures present. Have them record the sights, the smells, the temperature, and the humidity—anything that has to do with the sensory experience of being in that place at that time. Encourage them to use writing strategies to expand the piece, but have them resist the temptation to introduce humans or action into their scene.

In class, introduce a token object such as a shell, a piece of clothing, or any other unusual item (choose something that you are able to bring to the classroom), and have all students find a way to write that object into the setting they have described. It may be lying on the ground or hanging in a tree or half-buried in the dirt, whatever they choose.

Next, have them read with their peers to revise, clarify, and vivify the descriptions. Peers will give feedback and ask questions to help each other clarify the pictures they have constructed.

Following this peer work, have students introduce two characters who enter the scene and interact in some way with each other. Have students describe the characters as carefully as possible in order to give a picture and to allow the reader to distinguish between the two.

Finally, have students write a short narrative in which the characters in this setting encounter the token object and find a use for it. Depending upon the time you have available, you can have students share their narratives and discuss the uses found for the token object. It will also be helpful to reflect with the students on the process of writing effective description.

Conclusion

There are many other prereading exercises that you can do with your students, but I hope that you have found something here that will work for you to whet your students' appetites and engage them intellectually and emotionally with the themes they will encounter in *Lord of the Flies*. The next chapter will lead us through the text, scene by scene, with ideas to support an initial reading. Subsequent chapters will detail postreading study that leads students back into the text of *Lord of the Flies* to develop interpretations, cite textual evidence, support discussion and performance, engage writing for understanding, and complete individual or small group projects.

Chapter Materials

Name: _____   Date: _____

Student Activity Sheet #1:
You Under Pressure

Applicable Portion of the Novel: Prereading, All

Objectives:
1. Students will examine their own behavior in stressful situations.
2. Students will think critically about effective decision-making strategies and articulate their understanding through writing and discussion.

Common Core Standard(s): W.9-10.2 and W.9-10.10; W.11-12.10

Directions: Imagine yourself in the most stressful situation you have faced in your life. Try to recall how your behavior changed or was affected by the stress of that situation and note those changes below or in your journal. Describe examples of things you did or said that, upon reflection, were not what you would ordinarily do or say. In particular, write about how the stress affected your interaction with others. Finally, write what you would do differently if faced with a similar situation today.

Situation	Changes	What Would I Do Now?
Description:	1. 2. 3.	1. 2. 3.

General Reflection

_____

_____

_____

_____

Name: _____ Date: _____

Student Activity Sheet #2:
These Are Our Rules

Applicable Portion of the Novel: Prereading, All

Objectives:
1. Students will consider their own agency in determining the codes of their behavior, their individual positions in society, and their responsibilities to each other.
2. Students will generate rules of conduct for themselves and their peers and negotiate the adoption of those rules.
3. Students will interact with peers to solve problems respectfully.

Common Core Standard(s): SL.9-10.1; SL.11-12.1

Directions: The members of this class are going to create a society for themselves. As part of your charter, you have the freedom to set rules for yourselves. These rules will govern every aspect of your lives, from work to play to getting food and living arrangements.
1. Generate a list of rules that you would like your community to follow, and then prioritize that list from most important (1) to least important (10).
2. You will be assigned a small group to compare notes and discuss the lists with each other. Your group should come to consensus on 3–5 rules that you would adopt.
3. Come together as a class and choose one classmate to be leader. The leader may decide to adopt the rules by him or herself, or the leader may let the community vote for the rules that all adopt.
4. Discuss what the penalties will be for violation of each rule that the class has adopted. Discuss how those penalties will be enforced, or whether they can be enforced without threat of violence.
5. Reflect on the activity and what difficulties you faced.

_____

_____

_____

_____

_____

_____

_____

_____

_____

_____

_____

Student Activity Sheet #3:
Problem Situations

Applicable Portion of the Novel: Prereading, All

Objectives:
1. Students will project themselves into situations faced by the characters in *Lord of the Flies*.
2. Students will connect their own thinking in response to the problem situations with the decisions made by characters in *Lord of the Flies*.

Common Core Standard(s): SL.9-10.1; SL.11-12.1

Directions: Discuss the situation given to your group and generate possible responses to the questions asked. Once all groups have generated responses, we will discuss them as a class.

1. You discover that something a group of friends believes to be true, something that has caused conflict among them, is actually false. You want to share the new information with them, knowing that they may not believe you right away. Your friends are gathered at a party. Do you go straight to the party and tell all of them at once or do you wait and tell them individually?

   _____

   _____

   _____

   _____

2. You know someone who thinks of you as a friend, and you have spent time with him, although you find him annoying at times. He has made several attempts to be your friend, and you have been nice at times and not nice at other times. You witness another potential friend calling him names and punching him in the stomach. No adult is there to intervene. What are your options? What do you do?

   _____

   _____

   _____

   _____

3. You are in a setting with some kids your age and some younger kids, but no adults are present. You and the older kids are not paying attention to the younger kids, but you happen to notice that the younger kids are doing something that could be dangerous and cause them harm. What are your options? What do you do?

   _____

   _____

   _____

   _____

4. You are at a job, and the boss is not present. It is clear to you that not everyone is pulling his or her weight at work, and you are frustrated because it is causing more work for you, and you are behind already on your own work. What are your options? What do you do?

_____

_____

_____

_____

5. You have a job to do that is important to you and to your community. Everyone relies on you to do this job, but your friends are urging you to leave the job for a while and come with them to do something fun. You know your responsibility, but you also don't want to jeopardize your friendships. How do you decide what to do? Do you leave the job or say no to your friends?

_____

_____

_____

_____

6. You believe that a friend is too superstitious and is afraid of things you don't believe in, such as ghosts. You see that the person's fear is affecting his or her behavior. What are your options? What do you do?

_____

_____

_____

_____

7. You find that, due to a lack of judgment, you and your friends have done something that caused serious harm to another person. You believe that what you've done is wrong and you feel guilty for it. Some of your friends are making excuses and pretending that nothing happened. What are your options? What do you do?

_____

_____

_____

_____

Name: _____   Date: _____

Student Activity Sheet #4:
Good Leadership: What Does It Look Like?

Applicable Portion of the Novel: Prereading, All

Objectives:
1. Students will generate qualities they value in leaders.
2. Students will search for quotes and short readings on leadership, then share those quotes and ideas with the class.
3. Students will reflect on their own potential to lead.

Common Core Standard(s): SL.9-10.1 and RI.9-10.7; SL.11-12.1

Directions: Brainstorm qualities you like to see in leaders. Search online for quotes or short readings related to leadership. Ask your parents and other adults what they value in leaders. Bring your ideas to class and we will compare notes. Then we will generate a collection of leadership qualities and quotes to post on the classroom wall.

_____

_____

_____

_____

_____

_____

_____

_____

_____

_____

_____

_____

_____

_____

_____

_____

Lord of the Flies Movie Trailer

Note: All italicized passages are read by the narrator, typically the teacher.

Opening: Cue military music (for example, "The Haunter of the Dark" by Franco Cesarini or other music of the teacher's choosing).

Speaker		Sound effects
Narrator:	*A time of war. A group of boys, jettisoned from their airplane and scattered on an island.*	Explosion noise
Piggy:	What's your name?	
	Boys without supervision . . .	
Jack:	Aren't there any grownups?	
	Try to organize themselves . . .	Mumbles
Ralph:	We'd better all have names, so I'm Ralph.	
	And establish their roles . . .	
Piggy:	We got most names—	
Jack:	Shut up, Fatty!	
Ralph:	He's not Fatty, his real name's Piggy!	Laughter
	Small boys, frightened by what they don't understand . . .	
Small boy:	What about the beastie?	Mumbles
	And older boys, trying to calm them . . .	
Ralph:	But there isn't a beastie!	
	Set up a democratic society . . .	
Roger:	Let's vote for chief!	Cheers
	A call for order . . .	
Piggy:	Whoever has the conch gets to speak.	
	And consequences . . .	
Jack:	We'll have rules, lots of rules! Then when anyone breaks them–	
Maurice:	Bong!	
Bill:	Doink!	Cheers
	Then, a frightening realization . . .	
Piggy:	Who knows we're here? Nobody knows where we are!	
Ralph:	We'll have to look after ourselves.	
	A plan for rescue . . .	

Ralph:	We'll make a signal fire on the mountain!	
	And the desire for meat . . .	
Jack:	We'll hunt and kill and kill!	Cheers
	But soon, conflict arises . . .	
Ralph:	You let the fire go out!	
Jack:	We'll relight it!	
Ralph:	There was a ship! We could have been rescued!	
	And a new threat in the darkness . . .	
Samneric:	We saw the beast!	Frightened mumbles
	Strains the society . . .	
Piggy:	Are you sure?	
Simon:	Maybe it's only us . . .	
	As a power struggle erupts . . .	
Ralph:	I'm chief, I was chosen!	
Jack:	You can't hunt, you can't sing!	
	And the group splinters . . .	
Ralph:	Jack!	
Jack:	I'm not going to play any longer. Not with you!	
	The hunters dance . . .	
All:	(chanting) Kill the beast, cut his throat, do him in!	
	And a storm builds . . .	Thunder booms
All:	(chanting) Kill the beast, cut his throat, do him in!	
	Who will survive?	
All:	It's the beast! Ahhhh!	Screams
	This is William Golding's Lord of the Flies. *Coming to a class-room near you!*	

Cut music.

Student Activity Sheet #5:
Descriptive Writing Exercise

Applicable Portion of the Novel: Prereading, Chapter 1

Objectives:
1. Students will explore author's craft through sensory description writing.
2. Students will construct descriptive passages involving two characters and an object.
3. Students will familiarize themselves with the opening scene of *Lord of the Flies*.

Common Core Standard(s): W.9-10.3 and W.9-10.5; W.11-12.2 and W.11-12.3

Directions:
1. Find a natural setting (an outdoor space) and try to describe everything you see there in as much detail as possible. Immerse yourself in the plants, the animals, the insects, and the other objects or structures present. Record the sights, the smells, the temperature and the humidity—anything having to do with the sensory experience of being in that place at that time. Expand your writing however you see fit, but don't add humans to the setting.
2. Bring your draft to class, where you will receive a token object that you will need to write into your described setting. You may place the object anywhere in the setting.
3. Peers will give feedback and ask questions to help you clarify the picture constructed from language.
4. Following this peer work, introduce two characters who enter the scene and interact in some way with each other. Describe the characters as carefully as possible in order to give a picture and to allow the reader to distinguish between the two.
5. Finally, write a short narrative in which the characters in this setting encounter the token object and find a use for it.
6. Bring your completed scenes to class for sharing.

_____

_____

_____

_____

_____

_____

_____

_____

_____

_____

_____

_____

"I've got the conch": Reading *Lord of the Flies*

This chapter is designed to accompany you on a first reading of the book or, if you have read it before, to assist you in a preparatory reading prior to teaching the text. I suggest that you read this chapter piece by piece as you do that preparatory reading, and then perhaps return to it as you teach the initial reading to your students. The chapter offers a variety of discussion and journal topics, as well as a few reading strategies to enhance student understanding. The chapters of *Lord of the Flies* are divided here into sections, and each section is in turn discussed in detail.

When you begin the book with your students, you may have them make predictions about the book based on the title, *Lord of the Flies*, and the first chapter title, "The Sound of the Shell." Each of the chapters has a title, and they are worth discussing with your students. As each chapter is read in class, revisit the chapter titles in the afterglow of reading and ask students to make predictions based on the next chapter's title (see Chapter 6 for a writing activity related to Golding's draft titles for the book).

Now, without further ado, let's jump into the text of *Lord of the Flies*.

One: The Sound of the Shell

As mentioned above, I have divided each chapter into smaller sections and also into "units" or "beats," similar to dramatic scripts. Such separation will allow us to focus on individual scenes and transitions between them, rather than trying to discuss an entire chapter at a glance. I divide the first chapter into the following sections. You and your students may be able to further subdivide these scenes into smaller units:

1. Ralph and Piggy discover each other and the conch
2. Boys gather following the blowing of the conch
3. Boys discuss their situation, elect Ralph leader, and tease Piggy
4. Ralph, Jack, and Simon explore the island
5. Ralph, Jack, and Simon encounter a pig

The book opens with a description of "the boy with fair hair," who we later find out is Ralph. The description of his shirt sticking to him and his hair "plastered to his forehead" tells us we are in a hot, humid place, with a "scar smashed into the jungle," likened to a "bath of heat" (p. 1). As he descends the rocks, the boy scares up an exotic red and yellow bird, which emits a "witch-like cry" (p. 1), indicating a disturbance in nature, but also a potentially ominous nature disturbed. It is a different individual's voice that we first hear in the book, as he calls to the fair-haired boy from among the jungle creepers. Although "the boy with fair hair" becomes "the fair boy" before the end of the first page, the scene and both boys are portrayed as hot, sticky, and miserable. The second character's entrance is almost comic, as he backs out of the jungle in his greasy windbreaker. He is scratched by thorns, indicating that at least this part of the setting is hostile to humans. His physical features are described in details that set him apart from the fair boy: he is short and fat, with poor eyesight. The "fat boy" (p. 2) immediately looks for grownups, and the first conversation between the two demonstrates that, while the fair boy is processing where they are, the fat boy is trying to establish normalcy. The startled look on the fat boy's face at the fair boy's mention of no grownups is telling, too, as we will discover later in the text why the fat boy needs the protection of adults perhaps more than the other children. The fair boy, on the other hand, shows his glee at the prospect of no grownups by standing on his head, something he will do repeatedly at times of joy.

The dialogue between the two boys establishes backstory and context. They were on a plane, the pilot "dropped" them (p. 2), perhaps in some kind of an eject-able passenger cabin, or perhaps they just came down when the plane broke apart. Either way, they assume other kids have been scattered and that some were swept out to sea with the remains of the plane.

If this opening seems a bit implausible, it is important to note that we must accept the premise of the plane crash and the dispersal of the boys in order to move forward with the story. What will probably capture your students' attention more than the physical details of the setting or the unlikelihood of the situation is the tenor of the conversation between the fair boy and the fat boy. The fat boy is overly interested in establishing a friendship and gaining acknowledgment; the fair boy is not at all interested in the fat boy and wavers between indifference and overt insult. The fat boy asks the fair boy his name, and he replies, "Ralph" (p. 3), but does not ask the fat boy his name in return. He moves forward not only to reach the lagoon, but also to distance himself from the incessant talking of the fat boy. We learn that the fat boy has asthma, which keeps him from being able to run, and, as if he didn't have enough going against him, he suddenly suffers an episode of diarrhea. As the fat boy squats in the bush, Ralph runs away from him to the lagoon. Ralph strips down and his "golden" body (p. 5) stands naked in the hot sun. We are thus presented a dramatic contrast between the two: one fair, athletic, attractive, and healthy; the other overweight, asthmatic, nearsighted, and incontinent.

DISCUSSION/JOURNAL TOPIC: FIRST IMPRESSIONS

This spot in the story (p. 5) is a good place to stop reading and talk to your students about their images of these boys and their first impressions of the boys' personalities. It is also a good time to make sense of the setting and discuss how students picture it.

When the fat boy rejoins Ralph, he makes one of what will be several mis-judgments of others—misjudgments that will ultimately cost him his life. He is already thinking about organizing whatever boys they will find, and he mentions that they will have to get names. Ralph still doesn't ask him his name, so he hints that he hopes he won't have to retain the nickname he'd had at school. Ralph's sudden interest causes the fat boy to reveal that he was called "Piggy" (p. 6), and Ralph's reaction is both typical and merciless as he repeats the name over and over, laughing and pretend dive-bombing poor Piggy. Thus we learn that Piggy (and we will never learn his real name) has been the victim of teasing before, and yet his desperation to make friends leads him to make matters worse for himself. He promptly suffers another attack of diarrhea, which allows us as readers to get back into Ralph's reverie on the beauty of the island.

On page 7 we find a couple of paragraphs devoted to a description of the granite platform and lagoon that will become a central meeting place for the characters in the book. No descriptions in this book are accidental or gratuitous; they all have significance and weave in with the actions and dialogue of the characters. With this in mind, you may want to have your students report on how clear the descriptions of the platform and lagoon are for them, or whether they need help constructing a picture of the scene. Students can sketch what they see from the description and fill in the other landforms later in the chapter.

As Piggy reaches the platform, reluctantly takes off his clothes, and enters the water, he endures more overt rejection from Ralph. "Sucks to your auntie," and "Sucks to your ass-mar" (p. 8) are Ralph's brusque retorts when Piggy attempts to explain himself. Awkwardly, Piggy compliments Ralph on his swimming, even as he's absorbing verbal abuse from him. Students may comment on Piggy's tactics to gain access to his more attractive companion, but things deteriorate further for him when Ralph brags about his father, a commander in the Navy, and asks Piggy what his father does. Piggy's parents are dead, and his aunt operates a candy store. Also note that Piggy speaks with poor grammar, using phrases like "You can't half swim" (p. 8) and "Them fruit" (p. 4). These elements, taken with his grubby jacket, appear to establish a class difference between the two boys that makes Ralph even less interested in Piggy (Crawford, 2002).

But Piggy is a realist. When Ralph casually and confidently suggests that his father will rescue the boys, Piggy wastes no time poking holes in the theory. "How does he know we're here?" he asks (p. 9), and Ralph has no answer, only an internal monologue of "because, because, because" (p. 9). When Ralph finally suggests that his father would learn from the airport personnel, Piggy shares a piece of knowledge that further establishes context and changes this story at once from the typical lost-on-an-island boys' adventure. "Not them," Piggy says, "Didn't you hear what the pilot said? About the atom bomb? They're all dead" (p. 9). At this point, we do not know whether Piggy is a reliable source of such information, and the comment garners some consideration from Ralph, but not much. For Piggy, however, this is a realization that leads him to cry for the first time in the text.

ACTIVITY (SAS #7): FACTS ABOUT ATOMIC WEAPONS

Have your class do research on the Cold War and ask them to specifically seek information on atomic (i.e., nuclear) weapons. After they share their information in class, ask students whether the existence of nuclear weapons ever enters their conscious thoughts or whether they assume there is no current risk.

Clearly, Ralph thinks Piggy is a killjoy, and he pulls himself out of the water, trying to maintain the pleasant daydreams he's been having insofar as he can ignore Piggy. Piggy, for his part, is already thinking that they need to organize and find out how many others are on the island. "We got to do something," he says (p. 11). The two boys are worlds apart in their thinking, and it is at this point that the first object of note enters the story. Ralph spots something in the water that Piggy correctly identifies as a conch shell, and their shared efforts to extract the shell do for Piggy what his awkward jabbering could not do—bring him into affinity with Ralph. Piggy knows about conch shells. He has knowledge, which is a kind of social capital for him. While Ralph innocently examines and admires the shell, Piggy is already way ahead of him mentally, connecting the shell with the opportunity to call a meeting to bring together the survivors. When Ralph, after a few comic failed attempts, finds a way to use the conch as a horn, he scares up a flock of birds and "something [squeals] and [runs] in the undergrowth" (p. 13)—our first sign that there are pigs on the island.

It is at this point that the chapter shifts to the gathering of the boys, and Ralph and Piggy are connected not by a shared interest or affinity, but by the mere fact that they found each other first and blew the conch. As the first little boy comes forward and tells Piggy his name, Ralph is not interested in anything but blowing the conch. Golding's narrative describes the gathering of boys, and this presents an excellent opportunity for your students to examine how the boys are described and what the descriptions indicate about the boys' personalities.

ACTIVITY (SAS #8): CHARACTER CHARTS

Visualization of language used to describe characters can aid students in pulling together their understanding of the character relationships in *Lord of the Flies*. Have students choose one of the formats on SAS #8 at the end of this chapter and take notes throughout the unit, or post large charts on your classroom wall that allow for students to write comments on the characters. Use the descriptions to fuel classroom discussion, and use discussion to develop the charts.

Piggy appears effective in gathering names as Ralph continues to blow the conch, and thus society is established, until a large, dark figure is spotted on the beach. Much has been made of the first description of the choir: the uniformity, the word "creature" used to describe them from a distance, and the absurdity of the group that emerges when the "dark" mirage dissipates (p. 16). But the first appearance of Jack Merridew, the leader of the group and the principal antagonist in the book, is carefully drawn. His face is crumpled and freckled and "ugly without silliness" (p. 17). His face is described in almost inhuman terms, with eyes staring out of a face, ready to turn to anger. Ralph is complacent and welcoming, and after Jack demonstrates an unreasonable authority over the choir, making them keep line even in the hot sun, a boy faints (Simon), and we have a miniature portrait, a sort of Greek chorus-like preshow, of the turning point that will come with Simon's death later in the book. Also of note in this part of the scene is Piggy's immediate reaction to Jack, which is fear and retreat.

The scene shifts again as the meeting gets underway, with Jack and Ralph dominating the situation. When Jack calls for Piggy to "Shut up, Fatty," Ralph shares that his name is "Piggy," and everyone makes fun of him (p. 18). For students who have endured harassment and bullying themselves, this scene and the subsequent events may be difficult to discuss.

DISCUSSION/JOURNAL TOPIC: BULLYING

Discuss the treatment of Piggy in this scene. Have students discuss alternative ways that the boys could relate to Piggy. You may also bring in sources on bullying and its effects, or you can wait until later in the unit.

We get descriptions of the choir boys, including details associated with Roger (which your students will want to note) and Simon. When the idea of choosing a chief is mentioned by Ralph, the first conflict between Ralph and Jack is established. Their struggle for control will inform and drive the plot of the book. It is Roger who suggests a vote, a fact that will emerge as ironic by the book's end. At this point, Golding gives us a summary of characteristics of the principals: Piggy shows intelligence and Jack shows leadership capabilities, but Ralph has the conch, shows "stillness" (p. 19), and is good-looking. These factors, taken together, lead to his success. The fact that Ralph immediately gives Jack control of the choir, whose members Jack quickly turns into hunters, sets up the classic dichotomy between civil government and military leadership. Thus, Golding has constructed a minisociety, with its leadership and citizenry. Ralph and Jack look at each other with "shy liking" (p. 21), and a semihopeful tone is established.

DISCUSSION/JOURNAL TOPIC: PLAYING GAMES

The boys' first meeting is a comic version of an adult meeting, and one gets the sense that they are playing at it, except that the treatment of Piggy and the initial rivalry between Ralph and Jack are described seriously. Ask this question to your students: Are the boys playing or are they serious?

Ralph's next act as chief is to decide that he, Jack, and Simon must go explore their surroundings to determine whether they are in fact on an island, as they suspect. Ralph must extricate himself from Piggy, who confronts him over the ridicule he has endured because Ralph shared the humiliating nickname. Students may want to examine their exchange (pp. 22–23) to determine whether Ralph is gaining empathy for Piggy and whether his "genuine leadership" (p. 23) is legitimate based on his handling of the situation.

The chapter shifts again to the exploration of the setting and the discovery that they are in fact on an island. These few pages not only fill out the setting and introduce the ominous but immediately stimulating presence of large, balancing, movable rocks on the mountain, but they bring us close to the fun, careless exploring that characterizes earlier adventure stories, including, most notably, the main source for Golding's novel, Ballantyne's *The Coral Island* (see Chapter 2 of this book for a full discussion). The three boys are delighted with every challenge, they fall together wrestling in their delight, and they establish a camaraderie that may sustain them through their time on the island. When they stop their exploring to shove a large boulder off a cliff and watch it tumble down the mountain, it "smashes" a deep hole in the forest canopy. It is innocent fun for the boys, but they liken the dropping of the boulder to a "bomb" (p. 26), which calls to mind the war from which they have been evacuated. Also of note in this section is the patience with which Golding describes each element of the landscape and the description of what Simon calls the "candle buds" plant (p. 29) in particular. Rather than ending the scene once the boys have achieved their goal, Golding includes this curious exchange between the boys as they examine a strange-looking green plant. Simon's reaction to it—"candle buds"—establishes him as having a sense of beauty and a metaphorical aesthetic. Ralph's reaction is that of a pragmatist: "You couldn't light them," he says (p. 29). And Jack, who has slashed one with his knife, dismisses them "contemptuously," arguing, "We can't eat them" (p. 29). He then commands his companions to "come on" (p. 29). Thus, Jack still issues orders, even in Ralph's presence, and shows an antipathy toward the natural environment.

The final section of this chapter is only one page long, but it narrates a crucial event that will have repercussions throughout the story. As the boys encounter a baby pig caught up in the creepers, Jack poises himself to kill it, but hesitates, and the pig gets away. The taboo against shedding blood is apparent, and Golding's narrator acknowledges the understanding the boys have: "They knew very well why he hadn't" (p. 30). The chapter ends with Jack "daring" the other boys to contradict him in his assertion that "next time there would be no mercy" (p. 30).

Two: Fire on the Mountain

The second chapter moves the action forward and leaves us with the first tragic (albeit unconfirmed) death. I divide the chapter into the following units:

1. The second assembly: Ralph, Jack, and Simon report what they saw and stress the need for rules
2. The little boy with the mulberry birthmark mentions a snake-like "beastie," and debate follows
3. Ralph suggests the rescue fire, and the boys all leave; Piggy is disgusted
4. The gathering and building of the fire and the taking of Piggy's glasses
5. Piggy's standoff and the accidental fire

The first section of the chapter opens with a picture of the platform, crowded with boys, in the late afternoon sun, Ralph exerting his leadership with the conch. One major thread of this book is Ralph's evolving self-perception, and in this instance, he finds that he can fluently explain what he has to say. Unfortunately, as the scene and chapter move forward, Ralph finds himself struggling to focus his message and choose his words, relying on Piggy to provide logic, even if Piggy's outrage makes him difficult to listen to. The major characters' personalities are brought into sharper focus during this meeting, with Jack concerned only with hunting, food, and rules. When Ralph hints at the establishment of some parliamentary procedures, Jack says, "We'll have rules! Lots of rules! Then when anyone breaks 'em—" and the other boys chime in with "Whee—oh!", "Wacco!", "Bong!", and "Doink!" (p. 33), implying the need for physical punishment. Though we have already seen Jack's quick temper, his almost sadistic treatment of the choir, and his threatening mock stabs with his knife, here we see that the other boys are more than willing to go along with the idea of punishing offenders of the rules.

Piggy establishes himself as a sort of conscience for the group when he takes the conch and, on the verge of an asthma attack, reminds them that they have been shot down, that no one knows where they are, and that they may be there for a long time. In the way they respond to him the boys only view him as a killjoy, but they cannot ignore his words, and so it is Ralph who reaffirms, then reinterprets Piggy's words, following "So we may be here for a long time" with, "But this is a good island. We—Jack, Simon and me—we climbed the mountain. It's wizard. There's food and drink, and—." Then Jack says, "Rocks," and Simon says, "Blue flowers," before Piggy reminds them that Ralph has the conch (p. 34). As I've mentioned, nothing is an accident in this superbly formed book, so Jack's and Simon's choices of details to mention tell us about the mindset of each. Ralph says that they can have a "good time" until they get rescued, and then says, "It's like in a book" (p. 34). At once the boys bring up the names of *Treasure Island*, *Swallows and Amazons*, and *The Coral Island*, all books that were widely read in England in Golding's time, and books that *Lord of the Flies* parodies or condemns. Golding spoke about *The Coral Island* in interviews and has credited that book as providing the idea for his book (for a longer discussion of *The Coral Island*, see Chapter 2 of this book). Ralph reiterates generously that the island belongs to them and that it is "a good island" (p. 34).

Immediately, Jack grabs the conch, and a transition occurs, shifting us to the next unit in the chapter. When Jack mentions pigs and bathing water and wonders if anyone "found anything else" (p. 35), a small boy with a mulberry-colored birthmark on his face is more or less pushed forward and compelled to share what he has apparently been sharing with the other littluns. This scene is interesting in how the larger boys take different roles in assisting the small boy, with Piggy translating what the little boy whispers to him in his fright. What follows is the first volley in what will become the central catalyst in the eventual dissipation of their society: fear. Ralph's insistence that there is not a beast doesn't deter Piggy from repeating everything the little boy says, and Jack opportunistically claims that, if there is a "snake" (p. 37), then they'll hunt and kill it, offering himself as a protector. This is a scene to mark so that you can return to it with your students when they reach the final chapters of the book, to see the beginning of a pattern of how Jack uses fear to gain power. He is described through Ralph's perception of him: "The eyes that looked so intently at him were without humor" (p. 37). It is also noteworthy that Ralph, who sat calmly as a leader in the beginning of the chapter, loses his composure here and has to shout repeatedly that there is no beast. With the hint of terror in the air, Ralph, unable to convince everyone through logic that there is no beast, turns to the subject of rescue, and the chapter shifts again.

Ralph regains the respect and admiration of everyone but Jack when he speaks convincingly of rescue, and also when he expresses the original idea of building a signal fire on the mountaintop. At the first mention of a signal fire, the boys run off to the mountain, leaving Ralph and an indignant Piggy behind. As Ralph pursues the boys, Piggy is left again as the outsider. The scene shifts to the mountain, where Ralph has spotted a good pile of downed trees that should serve nicely to build a fire. As we will see more ironically in later chapters, common work builds friendships, as the boys share in the labor of gathering wood from the large pile. Jack is giving commands to the choir, and he and Ralph share another moment of camaraderie when they lift a large log together. Only Piggy is not involved in the common labor, something else that sets him apart throughout the book.

One sentence worth noting on page 40 comes in the second long paragraph, once the woodpile is nearly built and Ralph is standing on his head in pleasure. In describing the action, the narrator states, "Below them, boys were still laboring, though some of the small ones had lost interest and were searching this new forest for fruit." It is only once the wood is gathered and the twins, Sam and Eric (i.e., Samneric), add kindling that they realize they do not have means to start the fire. Jack realizes that they can use Piggy's glasses, but rather than asking for them, he physically snatches them off Piggy's head, an act of intimidation that everyone, in their desire to see the fruits of their labor, condones, including Ralph.

As the first fire rises and then fails, the scene shifts to the final developments of the chapter: Piggy's standoff and the accidental fire. The antagonism between Piggy and Jack grows, as Jack repeatedly tells Piggy to shut up, and Ralph tells Piggy to shut up as well. When Jack chastises Piggy for not helping build the fire, Simon steps in and acknowledges Piggy's role in bringing the glasses. Analysis of Simon should include all of these small details. Maurice shows intelligence by suggesting green twigs to maintain smoke, and Jack, eager to put himself in a position of providing for all, assigns the choir the responsibility of maintaining the fire as well as hunting for food. Other than Jack's intimidation of Piggy, another thing to notice in this section is the initial use of the word "savages," which is said by Jack: "After all, we're not savages. We're English, and the English are best at everything. So we've got to do the right things" (p. 44).

DISCUSSION/JOURNAL TOPIC: POWER

If your students show an interest in pursuing a line of inquiry related to power in the book, this is an excellent scene to discuss, as it shows how Ralph maintains the illusion of power while Jack subverts power by backing Ralph and making assignments.

Jack has not yet reached the point of violence, but we can see it stirring, especially in the way he tells Piggy to shut up. Piggy's "virtuous recrimination" (p. 45) is on the verge of being shouted down when he notices the smoke of the accidental fire and, I imagine somewhat sanctimoniously, says, "You got your small fire, all right" (p. 45).

Have students carefully examine this scene for strengths and weaknesses in Piggy's thinking and his method. What separates him from the others, and how does he move them forward? He is the bringer of bad news, not only because he is first to spot the accidental fire, but also because he reminds them, as they giggle with glee over setting the mountain on fire, that the littluns were playing down by the spot that is now burning. Piggy clearly suffers an asthma attack as he realizes that the boy with the mulberry mark is missing, and it is as though the other boys cannot comprehend the reality that Piggy is forcing them to acknowledge. Ironically, it is Piggy's own incompetence in counting the littluns that leaves us unsure of how many deaths may have occurred in the fire. The chapter ends with an eerie dread spreading among the boys.

Three: Huts on the Beach

At this point in the book there is a break, as some time has passed between the accidental fire and the opening scene of Chapter 3. We know this because the description of Jack in the opening sentences mentions that his hair is considerably longer than it had been when they arrived on the island. A perceptive reader will look for other signs of changes that have taken place in the boys and their surroundings.

In many ways this chapter belongs to Jack, as Golding takes us inside his psyche while he hunts and reveals his changing outward self as a result of time spent on the island and his frustration at not succeeding in killing a pig. For students who may later write explicitly about Jack, this is an important chapter to mine for evidence. But the chapter also focuses on Jack and Ralph as potential friends and allies, and describes the opening rift between them over unshared priorities. Finally, the chapter takes us with Simon as he feeds the littluns and retreats into his secret place, presumably to sleep.

I prefer to separate the chapter into the broad divisions suggested below.
1. Jack alone, hunting
2. Jack, Ralph, and Simon talking by the shelters
3. Ralph and Jack on the beach, looking at the fire, then returning to the shelters
4. Simon and the littluns
5. Simon retreats to his bower

The first segment of the chapter opens with a detailed description of Jack hunting, and Golding puts us in the moment by engaging all senses, portraying the stillness of a boy completely focused on his pursuit. The forest, the heat, and Jack's stillness are presented in detailed description. Golding even spends two sentences describing a pile of pig droppings that Jack finds. These first few paragraphs provide an excellent example of text to use for both comprehension work and inference work. We learn from the physical description of Jack that some time has passed, enough for his hair to grow and bleach out, and enough for his skin to grow darker and chronically burned. His clothes, a signifier of civilization, have been reduced to rags. Have students look for clues of Jack's mental state as well, and have them explain why Golding likens him to a dog, to an ape, or to a "furtive thing" (p. 51). Jack has also obviously learned great patience in the hunt, but we will see that he doesn't have any patience for society. The word "mad" in the sense of mental instability is used repeatedly, as is the word "frustration" (p. 51). On the other hand, Jack shows great discipline and patience in this scene, patience that will eventually pay off for him and change his position in the society of boys. But for now, he remains frustrated as he flings his spear unsuccessfully at a pig, then returns to the platform to join the other boys.

The first shift in the chapter occurs when Jack greets Ralph, who is working with Simon to erect shelters. As we know that time has passed, we can also assume that the shelter work has been going on for some time, and Ralph seems to show the same kind of focus on his task as Jack showed on his, not even noticing Jack's arrival, he is so intent on what he is doing. But after he does notice Jack, he makes an unsuccessful attempt to move a branch into place for the shelter and almost immediately shows his frustration, flinging himself down to the ground. The conversation that follows tells the story of what has been happening since the accidental fire that ended the previous chapter. Ralph complains about the laziness of the other boys (all except Simon), and shows signs that he is irritated by Jack's obsession with hunting. The society of boys has made plans and rules, and, as Ralph admits, they love meetings, but the plans and the rules are not working out so well. Tension between Ralph and Jack comes to the surface almost right away. The dialogue between them on pages 53 and 54 would make for a great classroom drama workshop.

ACTIVITY (SAS #10): STAGING CONFLICT

Take the dialogue between Jack and Ralph on pages 53 and 54, write it out as speeches in a script, and then take the narration and format it as stage directions. The conversation vacillates between friendly, casual talk and angry, resentful arguing. Have students perform the scene and workshop it as a class.

Jack and Ralph parallel each other in their anger, with Ralph talking about shelters and Jack talking about meat. The narrator indicates the subtext of their words: "They were both red in the face and found looking at each other difficult" (p. 54). There's a shift in the conversation when Ralph breaches the topic of the boys' fear. Simon's interruption startles both Ralph and Jack, as he refers to the horrors of the previous chapter and the unmentionable snake-thing. These boys are trying to make sense of fear, and though Jack says the boys are "batty" (p. 55), they all agree that they need shelters for a "home" (p. 55). Jack goes on to describe the way he feels sometimes while hunting, and it is important to note that Jack is essentially acknowledging his own fear. When he stops and Ralph tells him to go on, Jack clearly admits to the feeling of being hunted, but then Ralph, having given Jack license to be honest, dismisses what Jack says with, "Well, I don't know" (p. 56). Jack, showing his intensity once more, ends that part of the conversation with, "Only I know how they feel. See? That's all" (p. 56).

Ralph's response demonstrates a sense of fear as well, as he brings up the subject of rescue, and Jack cannot immediately remember what Ralph is talking about. Strangely, Jack ties rescue to the hunting of pigs, saying that he'd like to be rescued, but he'd like to kill a pig first. Golding gives us the "opaque, mad look" (p. 56) in Jack's eyes again, and Ralph reminds him that the hunters have agreed to keep the signal fire going. The next section of the chapter begins with the boys running down the beach to check on the signal fire. It doesn't take long for them to start openly arguing again, as Jack is still clearly focused on hunting, whereas Ralph is more desperate in his desire to be rescued. Ralph mistakes Jack's "Got it!" (p. 57) as a sign that he has spotted a ship, when Jack is thinking only of how to find and kill a pig. This exchange prefigures the crisis in the following chapter, when a ship does come by and the fire is out. Ralph's complaint about Jack not "noticing" the shelters (p. 57) underscores the immaturity of the boys. Jack has taken on a masculine hunter-gatherer role while Ralph has taken on a feminine domestic role, and he sounds like an underappreciated housewife when he complains that at least Jack likes his work.

At this point, the boys look around and notice the other boys (including, notably, Piggy) not helping, but just lying around, staring into the water. The boys seem to be learning about people. Any part of this section of the chapter can provide material for interpretation and conversation, from Jack's offer to help with the shelter and Ralph's reply of "Don't bother" (p. 57), to their shared assessment of Simon as both helpful and "queer" (p. 57), to Golding's description of the growing distance between the two as "two continents of experience and feeling, unable to communicate" and "in love and hate" (p. 58). As this section of the chapter ends, they are boys again, laughing and splashing in the pool. Ask your students how they perceive the relationship between the two boys at this point, and who has the better arguments.

DISCUSSION/JOURNAL TOPIC: MEAT OR RESCUE?

Have students imagine themselves on the island with these boys. Would they see themselves as more interested in finding meat or in getting rescued? Why?

I like to think of the remaining sections of the chapter as a sort of coda as we part ways with Jack and Ralph and follow Simon through the forest. The description of Simon parallels the description of Jack that opens the chapter, and it is told in as much detail and with as much patience. But Simon is not hunting, and although the other boys see him as mad, Golding does not apply that adjective to him. Simon's eyes are "bright" (p. 59) rather than opaque, as Jack's are.

This three-page vignette of Simon feeding the children and retreating to his secret bower makes a great study piece. The narrative is thick with almost painstaking description, first of Simon himself, then of his scene with the littluns, and finally, of the deep forest bower he enters secretly, presumably to sleep. What is worth noticing here? First, Simon's air of intent as he walks up the scar and toward the forest. Second, the fact that the littluns pursue him, perhaps knowing he will feed them, as he probably has before. This feeding of the littluns alludes to the Biblical story of Christ feeding the masses with loaves and fishes (Olsen, 2000). Third, the littluns' speech, which is described as unintelligible. Fourth, the "booming" and "roar" of bees in the "ripeness" (p. 59) of the fruit bushes. Fifth, Simon's uncomplaining gesture of feeding the children until they are satisfied—something that would be unusual to imagine any of the other larger boys doing. Sixth, after leaving the littluns, Simon's "almost furtive" (p. 60) movements before entering his bower. The same word was used to describe Jack hunting at the beginning of the chapter and Roger in the opening chapter. In fact, had Jack been hunting at that moment near where Simon hides, we can assume that he might blindly hurl a spear at Simon, wishing to stick a pig. Of course, he will do more than that to Simon later, with the help of the others.

The description of Simon's bower may be especially difficult for students to picture, as the average teen doesn't know what creepers are, and may not be able to imagine how lush and overly fertile the place is.

ACTIVITY (SAS #11): COLLAGE OF TROPICAL VEGETATION

Have students find at least two pictures of jungle or tropical island scenery and bring them to class. Create a class collage of images and post it near the Wall of Notable Quotes. Have students comment on the photos they found and what in the story those images bring to mind.

Again, nothing in this book appears by accident, and it will be worth spending a little time picturing the place with your students. As Simon settles in, we share his shifting focus to the sounds of the island, and yet the loudest sound is apparently the "susurration" (p. 61) of his own blood. Remember that he is the boy who fainted, and here we have the next reference to his emotional state (something that will crescendo with his hallucination scene in Chapter 8 of the novel). What we are left with here is a peaceful and separated space for this boy who demonstrates a canny and generous nature, a plainness of speech, and a grasp of humanity that necessitates his otherness. Simon, unlike the others, sleeps in a peaceful "cabin" (p. 60) of plants, surrounded by beautiful night flowers. Thus the chapter ends.

This is a great spot in the book, following minor conflicts but before the major crises that will determine the book's outcome, for you to work with your students to describe the major characters, their qualities, and their conflicts. Use the character charts described in SAS #8 (see page 106).

Four: Painted Faces and Long Hair

The fourth chapter in *Lord of the Flies* delivers a crisis and a progression of stress that leads to violence. The chapter can be divided into the following units or movements, each of which can be further subdivided for purposes of discussion or comprehension focus.

1. A summary of the boys' situation
2. A focus on three littluns, Roger, and Maurice
3. Henry on the beach and Roger throwing the rocks
4. Jack paints his face
5. Ralph and Piggy: an uneasy relationship
6. Ralph sees the ship and runs to the mountain
7. Confrontation between Ralph, Jack, and Piggy on the mountain
8. The boys roast and eat a pig

One of the benefits of dividing the chapter into these shorter movements is that teachers can then use the divisions to structure class discussion or to assign small groups for closer analysis. You can jigsaw the groups to create mini-expert readings to be shared out in a student-centered workshop.

ACTIVITY (SAS #12): JIGSAW FOR CHAPTER 4

After students have read Chapter 4, have them convene in eight different groups, then assign to each group one of the eight divisions in the chapter, as identified above. Each group will discuss their chosen section of the chapter and generate interpretive statements of what the section is about. Then reconfigure into larger groups, each one having a representative of each of the smaller groups. Students in these second groups will take turns sharing with their peers the interpretive statements from the smaller groups.

The first section of this chapter marks a departure from the storytelling mode of the early chapters in that it pulls away to give us a long view of the boys and their situation. Whereas each of the first three chapters started in a moment (the first two with a focus on Ralph and the third with a close-up shot of Jack), Chapter 4 summarizes the rhythms of the days and nights on the island, giving the impression that each day is similar to the others. The different characteristics of morning, midday, early evening, and night are described principally through their effects on the boys' emotional states. Nature is not benignly benevolent, but harsh and difficult, with snapping sharks, oppressive sunshine, and dangerous plants that cut and scrape those who climb on them.

One thematic feature that stands out in the description of the boys, and especially the littluns, is the ignorance that informs their state of being. During the pleasant mornings, "play was good and life so full that hope was not necessary and therefore forgotten" (p. 62). Rather than seeking to understand the mirages that appear in the midday sun, the boys "ignored them, just as they ignored the miraculous, throbbing stars" (p. 62). They obviously ignore their own filthiness, and as we learn later, they also ignore Ralph's rules regarding where they should relieve themselves.

As evening sets in, another time of "coolness" approaches, but it is "menaced by the coming of the dark" (p. 63)—a narrative comment that indicates the consistency of the boys' fears. Golding's narrator sums up the succession of days with reference to the "northern European tradition of work, play, and food right through the day" (p. 63). The first individual portrait drawn against this summary backdrop is of young Percival, the littlest of the littluns, who appears through his erratic behavior to have lost contact with reality. Percival is miserable, and we will see shortly how his status among the littluns mirrors Piggy's status among the biguns. If we choose to approach this story as a parable of education, we see how the behavior of the biguns is sloppily recreated among the littluns, just as the behavior of adults is reflected in the conflicted society of the biguns.

Golding summarizes the lives of the littluns using unpleasant details, explaining that they have "chronic diarrhoea," "suffered untold terrors," and are "filthily dirty" (p. 63). You can discuss the summary description of the littluns with your class, leading them to contemplate why Golding includes it at all. Although they cry for their mothers and huddle together in the night, their lives are described as "passionately emotional" and "corporate" (p. 64), marked by typical fantasies of building sand castles and populating their make-believe world with elements of the civilization they have left behind. Golding's littluns, assumed to be around age 6, might appear to contemporary readers to act more like 3- or 4-year-olds. They are apparently incapable of conversation, and experience the world with very little comprehension.

The first shift in the chapter occurs with the line "Three were playing here now" (p. 64), which brings us out of summary mode and into a dramatic situation. Henry is introduced, and the narrator makes reference to the fact that he is distantly related to the boy with the mulberry-colored birthmark who disappeared in Chapter 2 of the novel. Your students may wonder why the presumably dead boy is mentioned in this context. The narrator makes the point that Henry does not seem to comprehend the implications of his missing relative. Percival, Piggy's parallel in the littluns' world, is described as "mouse-colored" and unattractive "even to his mother" (p. 64). Johnny, who possesses a "natural belligerence" (p. 64), may be a parallel for Jack, or perhaps Roger.

Enter two biguns, Roger and Maurice, who so casually walk through the littluns' sand castles and destroy them that we can assume that they relish in it. We are given the first of what will be many subtle depictions of the boys' fading sense of English morality through Maurice's mumbled excuse for getting sand in Percival's eyes. Maurice literally and figuratively trots away from his discomfort over plain meanness. But Maurice's act becomes a tutorial in bullying for Johnny, who flings sand into Percival's eyes until he cries. The scene shifts to Roger, and a new section of the chapter begins as Henry walks to another part of the beach.

We may notice that the shift in focus from character to character serves to make the narrative function like a wandering camera, moving from one part of the island to the next, from one boy to the next, stopping to tune in to selected actions. The focus of the third section in this chapter is Henry, who is being watched by Roger. Henry's encounter with the "tiny transparencies" (p. 65), little beach scavengers in the foam of the tide, demonstrates two things: First, that the transparencies themselves represent an example of nature's course, "scavenging" like "tiny teeth in a saw" for any "detritus" that they might encounter (p. 65); and second, that Henry, in his manipulation of these creatures, experiences the happy thrill of "exercising control over living things" (p. 66). The actions are layered here, with the littlun trying to control (terrorize) nature and the bigun attempting to terrorize the littlun.

Teachers may choose to focus on this section of Chapter 4 as an illustration of Roger's descent into amorality, and the scene provides an opportunity to explore the concept of the taboo. Roger gets the idea to throw rocks around Henry, presumably from witnessing the coconuts falling around himself. Henry may have been Roger's ally if he were a bigun, but as a littlun, he is easy prey, and the description of Roger hiding behind the tree, "breathing quickly, his eyelids fluttering" (p. 67) provides a great conversation opportunity for your students.

Discussion/Journal Topic: Cruelty—Does It Come Naturally, or Is It Learned?

Have students discuss the scene in Chapter 4 with the littluns on the beach and the entrance of Maurice and Roger. Is the behavior of the boys natural or learned? Have students reflect on their own experience.

One other detail in this little scene that may blow by your students, but that is worth considering, is the narrative sentence "Roger's arm was conditioned by a civilization that knew nothing of him and was in ruins" (p. 67). The conditioning relates to his aiming to miss, the taboo against harming others still echoing from Roger's civilized childhood, as explained in the sentences that precede this one. But the end of the sentence is the narrator's affirmation of Piggy's knowledge. Whether or not there actually was a nuclear attack, as Piggy recalled hearing a man say, if we have no reason to doubt the veracity of our narrator (and I believe we do not), then "ruins" is a fair description of the world the boys left behind. And yet the boys never have a conversation about the possibility of a destroyed homeland. Your students may wish to discuss the implications of this narrative statement.

The shift between this section of the chapter and the next happens with the sudden and seemingly prescient appearance of Jack. "Roger," he says (p. 67), just as Roger has done something on the verge of evil, and neither we nor Roger know whether Jack has witnessed Roger's act of incipient cruelty. Jack appears almost supernaturally, but he wastes no time commenting on Roger's behavior, as he is focused on another goal: disguising himself for the hunt. It is curious that Samneric are part of this scene, but given what happens later in the chapter (and in the book), their presence is necessary. When they "protest timidly about something" (p. 68), I assume it has to do with tending the fire, as Jack's response ("No. You two come with me," p. 68) doesn't make much sense unless Samneric are trying to leave the scene. The detail with which Golding narrates Jack's actions, from trying once and failing to make a painted mask, to succeeding, demonstrates the realism in the story that offsets its more symbolic or metaphorical elements.

The painting of Jack's face provides yet another opportunity for students to explore human nature through the book. The transformation in Jack is immediate and fearsome.

> He knelt, holding the shell of water. A rounded patch of sunlight fell on his face and a brightness appeared in the depths of the water. He looked in astonishment, no longer at himself but at an awesome stranger. He split the water and leapt to his feet, laughing excitedly. Beside the pool his sinewy body held up a mask that drew their eyes and appalled them. He began to dance and his laughter became a bloodthirsty snarling. He capered toward Bill, and the mask was a thing on its own, behind which Jack hid, liberated from shame and self-consciousness. The face of red and white and black swung through the air and jigged toward Bill. Bill stared up laughing; then suddenly he fell silent and blundered away through the bushes. (pp. 68–69)

"The mask compelled them" (p. 69) ends this section with the narrator's flip analysis of their behavior.

Discussion/Journal Topic: The Lucifer Effect

Have students discuss the effect of anonymity on people's willingness or inclination to commit violent acts. How does wearing a mask or painting our faces "free" us to hurt others? Or does it? Are there instances when wearing a mask is a good thing? Use Philip Zimbardo's book *The Lucifer Effect* as a resource for discussion.

The next section of the chapter shifts us away from Jack and the hunters, and away from the littluns, to our other major characters, reiterating the painful reality of Piggy's outsider status. This scene presents a repeat of Piggy's painful attempts to gain Ralph's friendship and also underscores the boys' inability to interpret each other. This section provides the opportunity to continue considering Piggy's character and his situation. Focusing students on what makes Piggy an outsider allows them to find clues in the section that explain or illustrate his status (hair, accent, fat, asthma, laziness). Ralph ends the conversation abruptly when Piggy mentions rescue, telling Piggy to "shut up" (p. 70). This comment aligns Ralph with Jack more so than with Piggy. Ralph separates himself from Piggy just to avoid the annoyance, but it is ironic that shortly after Piggy mentions rescue, Ralph happens to spot a ship on the horizon. At this point, the focus changes once more.

The reactions of the boys present, and their subsequent discovery of the extinguished signal fire, read like a slow-motion film. Walk students through this scene and have them note the separate behaviors of the characters during this crisis. Simon immediately sees things from Ralph's perspective and tries to comfort him, although Simon himself experiences strong emotions, screaming Ralph's name and crying by the time they reach the spot on the mountain where the fire should be burning. Piggy, naturally, cannot see well enough to spot the boat, and relies on Ralph to provide information—something Ralph is unable to do. Maurice provides a figure of incompetence, unable even to put his pants on in the excitement. As soon as Ralph realizes that there is no fire burning, he does what his limited intellectual resources tell him to do, which is to try to run to where the fire should be. Golding includes here small details that are easily missed. One such detail is the "complex undergrowth" that covers the scar made by their crash landing (p. 72). This is important not only because it indicates that time has passed and the island is reclaiming the physical landscape, but also because that undergrowth slows Ralph in a time of crisis. The undergrowth could be discussed as purely physical or metaphorical, representing the boys' society.

Ralph faces dilemmas such as having to choose whether to run on or to wait for Piggy, the bringer of the lighting glasses. He experiences a moment on the cliff, having discovered the spot where the fire went out, when he runs back and forth screaming for the ship to come back. Ralph's confusion and utter helplessness in this moment parallel Golding's description of a Neanderthal man in *The Inheritors* when he encounters the violence of Homo Sapiens for the first time. Ralph's anger, as indicated when he "reached inside himself for the worst word he knew" (p. 73), can be compared to Piggy's bumbling panic, Simon's sadness, and Maurice's lack of comprehension.

DISCUSSION/JOURNAL TOPIC: WHAT SHOULD THEY DO?

What should the boys do when they find that the signal fire is out? How does the knowledge that a ship has passed affect the situation? What could the boys do immediately to help their situation? What should they do in the long run?

The scene shifts again, setting up the climax of the chapter, when Ralph spots the hunters returning to the signal fire spot. The boys are presented as returning from a successful hunt, apparently aided by the anonymity of their masks. For his part, Jack is very excited to tell Ralph about the hunt. The words spoken and the descriptions that accompany them extend our knowledge of Jack's, Ralph's, and Piggy's personalities. Jack's natural exuberance descends into quick anger, Ralph's frustration takes away his ability to reason properly, and Piggy opens himself to attack by virtue of his false assumption that Ralph will protect him. This scene gives students (and all readers) a great deal to think about, process, and discuss. Your students may want to focus on Ralph's leadership, Jack's glorification of the killing (which is compared to "a long satisfying drink," p. 76), Simon's "passions" (p. 78), or Piggy's mistreatment. They may also want to consider how the boys could have addressed the situation more successfully than they did.

ACTIVITY (SAS #13): BLOCKING THE CONFRONTATION ON THE MOUNTAIN

This scene makes a good candidate for *blocking*, the theatre process of mapping out movements of characters as they speak with one another. I would suggest reading this section (starting with the return of the hunters) aloud with the students, and then having them work in small groups to reread the passage and trace out the movements of the characters.

Blocking the scene will ease the students into addressing the difficult topic of Jack's violence toward Piggy and the subtler, complicated feelings between Ralph and Jack. Jack is exuberant and thrilled when he arrives, and it takes him some time to understand the crisis. Ralph, for his part, is unwilling to acknowledge the success of the hunters, so offended is he with the disobedience of his followers. Jack has been giving orders that contradict Ralph's wishes, and it is clear, to use Samneric as an example, that the other boys aren't willing to cross Jack, even if it means disobeying Ralph's orders.

A good focus sentence is: "There was the brilliant world of hunting, tactics, fierce exhilaration, skill; and there was the world of longing and baffled commonsense" (p. 76). If you were a kid, which world would you choose?

Five: Beast From Water

This chapter contains more dialogue than other chapters, and we are allowed to hear more voices than in any other chapter. What is significant in all the talking is that the assembly was designed by Ralph to "put things straight" (p. 86) following the problem of the fire going out, but what results from the debate is a deepening sense of disorder, conflict, and fear. The chapter contains several distinct scenes, divided as follows.

1. Ralph's reflection on the assembly
2. Ralph's opening speech
3. Jack's speech and Piggy's speech
4. The littluns' speeches
5. Simon and the ghost debate
6. Ralph, Piggy, and Simon after the assembly breaks apart

These divisions, although based on definite shifts in the focus of the narrative, could be further subdivided. A good exercise for your students would be to take a chapter or a section of a chapter and ask them to define the shifts in narrative focus or spots where the storytelling changes, moving from real time to analysis or summary.

The first section of the chapter, Ralph's reflection, reveals Ralph's limitations with language and a vague recognition that he is a child ill-equipped to exercise adult authority.

DISCUSSION/JOURNAL TOPIC: RALPH'S STRUGGLE

Have your students read the first three paragraphs of Chapter 5, ask them to pick out what they think is the most important sentence or phrase, and then discuss why they picked what they did. Ask students to what extent they identify or do not identify with Ralph in this moment, and whether they themselves have experienced "the wearisomeness of this life" (p. 83). You may also ask students why Ralph breaks into a trot at after he realizes how filthy he is (p. 84). I see that gesture as a sign of panic starting to rise within Ralph.

Golding is meticulous, as always, in his description of the essential incompetence of the boys, as revealed through Ralph's realizations—for example, the "irregular and sketchy" (p. 84) quality of everything the boys make and the continued tolerance of the ridiculous unbalanced log. We also get a sense of Ralph's limitations, particularly with language. Ralph realizes that "Piggy could think" (p. 85), and he cannot. With that thought, he takes the conch and blows it, which brings this section of the chapter to a close.

ACTIVITY (SAS #14): APPRECIATING GOLDING: A LESSON IN DESCRIPTIVE WRITING

On pages 84–86 of *Lord of the Flies*, the narrator describes the assembly platform as it appears to Ralph in the evening. Have students count the number of sentences that describe the platform, how many sentences describe the thoughts of Ralph, and how many tell of an action occurring. Then ask students to narrate a story with three to five events, even if those events are as small as someone moving an arm or taking a step. Between each movement, the writer must include three to five sentences of description.

The next section of the chapter begins as the boys gather for the assembly following Ralph's blowing the conch. This section and those that follow allow your students an opportunity to explore the concepts of rhetoric and persuasion. You may direct them to read with the goal of evaluating the arguments made by each of the speakers, then choosing whom they would follow in the situation. It seems that Ralph has worked out several points, which he will make against an unruly group. Golding's structure in this scene is similar to Shakespeare's structure in the funeral oration scene in *Julius Caesar*, where we have leaders speaking and the crowd vocalizing their response from time to time. In this scene, the group as a whole functions as a sort of Greek chorus that reacts to every point made by the leader. The sniggers, boos, and laughter that echo Ralph's various statements allow us to experience narrative drama, and this chapter is an excellent one for students to translate into a script and act for each other (See Chapter 5 of this book), mainly to experience audibly the group's reactions to what is said.

Ralph knows that whatever he says will get twisted by the "practiced debaters" (p. 86), but he is determined to say all that's on his mind, even if his words bring out the immaturity of the boys, who "roar" with laughter at the mention of being "taken short" (p. 88). Ralph in this scene is like a teacher with no classroom management skills, who must tolerate the continuous noise of students who do not respect his position and who are tired of his relentless focus on rescue. Sensing this, it is no surprise that Ralph resorts to rhetorical questions ("Is a fire too much for us to make?" p. 88) and hyperbole ("Can't you see we ought to—ought to die before we let the fire out?" p. 88). As he gets shouted down by the crowd of boys who believe his rules are excessive, Ralph's panic comes back ("Too many things," p. 89), and he leaps up on a trunk in order to be heard. While Ralph's first rules regarding keeping fresh water, only using one place for a toilet, and keeping the fire going are reasonable, he steps beyond his reasonable authority by requiring the boys to climb the mountain to cook their food. At this point, when he is first in jeopardy of losing control, he brings up the topic that will dominate the following three chapters: fear. He ends his speech and allows others to talk, marking a shift to the next section in the chapter.

It should not be surprising to your students that Jack leaps up first to speak, though Piggy has already tried to grab the conch. In Jack's speech we see the kind of leadership that presents a threat to Ralph. He belittles others for their fear while acknowledging his own. He inspires confidence through might, and resorts to name-calling, labeling the littluns "cry-babies and sissies" (p. 90). Students may note that, at this point, Jack does not debate the points Ralph has made, but addresses the topic Ralph has opened for discussion. The crowd continues to function as a reactive chorus during this speech and the others, so we are able to gauge how they are receiving the speakers' messages by the descriptions of their reactions. Jack, by seizing the opportunity to identify himself as the first line of defense against an unknown threat ("Am I a hunter or am I not?" p. 91), begins to establish a personal legend that will allow him to ascend to the brutal dictatorship he enjoys in the book's final chapters. After all, it is only he who has been every-where on the island and it is he who has killed to bring them food. As the narrator says, "The whole assembly applauded him with relief" (p. 91). For students wishing to develop a political reading of the book, here is the beginning of the military coup d'état, made possible through the glamorization of the warrior.

When Piggy takes the conch, the tone shifts and the testosterone generated by Jack's warrior speech inspires the chorus to rain down insults on Piggy, which he bears in order to deliver his message on the "scientific" nature of life (p. 92). Rather than reacting to his logic, the crowd reacts to his words and uses them against him. He offers them a logical way to alleviate their fears of a beast, but he also opens up the possibility of fear of each other—something he has a right to contemplate, given his treatment thus far in the book. Although the assembly could have ended here, Piggy, unwisely, suggests that they let the littluns speak about their fears as a way of proving them (scientifically) incorrect. Thus, the next shift in the chapter takes place.

As I have mentioned, any section of any chapter of this book can be examined as a microcosm of the novel, because every scene is interrelated. The first littlun, Phil, recounts his dream to the fascinated audience, and creates a ministudy in the power of storytelling. Golding creates drama by reminding us that they are in relative darkness: "The child's voice went piping on from behind the white conch" (p. 93). The image of a disembodied voice brings forth the suspense and fear that the child experienced. Consequently, Ralph's protests that the child was only dreaming or sleepwalking do not convince the other boys, and it is not until Simon confesses that he has been out walking at night that the fantasy created by Phil's story dissipates. But this is only the first of two tales by littluns, and the next, which introduces us fully to Percival Wemys Madison, isn't as easily dismissed.

What do we notice about Percival's little scene? Is it surprising that the boys almost immediately taunt him with the chant of "What's your name? What's your name?" (p. 95) when he is too shy to speak up? Like any good boy, the littlun has memorized his personal information, but he has already forgotten his telephone number, the first sign that he is losing his grip on his former life. Remember that it is Percival who has appeared the most homesick of all the boys, and in this instance his loud sorrow is contagious; it is only Maurice in his cleverness who saves the assembly from being drowned in the littluns' tears. As Percival collects himself enough to whisper to Jack, we see another hint of the brilliance of Golding's storytelling. No one but Jack hears Percival's comment, but they all, especially Ralph, appear interested in what he says. Jack eventually releases Percival, who quickly falls asleep while Ralph awaits Jack's report of what he said. Finally, "Jack cleared his throat, then reported casually. 'He says the beast comes out of the sea'" (p. 97).

What is extraordinary about this subtle exchange is that we don't know whether Jack is faithfully reporting Percival's comment, or whether he is injecting his own comment. After students have completed the book, this will be a great spot to return to, to get students' take on it. The time that Jack takes to clear his throat, and the casual tone of his report may lead some students to believe that Jack is here injecting fear into the situation, perhaps for his own gain. If any students draw attention to these lines in the first read-through of the book, you should be pleased, because it means they are engaged in interpreting Jack. On the other hand, if they have not read the rest of the book, they will not be ready to argue one interpretation or the other with any authority. So bookmark it for later.

DISCUSSION/JOURNAL TOPIC: PERCIVAL'S STORY: WHAT ARE THE EFFECTS?

How are the boys influenced by Percival's story and his crying? Why do you think they were influenced as they were?

Mention of the beast's coming from the sea leads Maurice to boast that he knows (via his father) that not all animals in the sea have been discovered yet. It is here that the issue of fear begins to take on a physical structure, and the argument, guided by fantasy, grows loud and unruly, much to Ralph's dismay. In this way, the stage is set for Simon to shift the focus of the debate and the chapter.

By this point in their reading, your students may be tired of the extensive dialogue and frustrated by the difficulty of identifying speakers when Golding doesn't clearly say who is speaking. This difficulty increases as darkness falls on the assembly. Simon's assertion on page 98 that there may be a beast, and that "maybe it's only us," is a pivotal line in the book. Unfortunately for Simon, he is unconvincing, due to his own dread of public speaking and Piggy's immediate rejection of his idea. It is ironic that Piggy had voiced nearly the same thought earlier in the chapter, yet he is unwilling or unable to acknowledge Simon's perception (despite the fact that this is how Piggy feels about Jack). Simon feels more deeply than any of the boys, and his deep feelings paralyze him in debate, despite his uncanny ability to speak the plain truth.

After an unnamed individual suggests that Simon may have been saying that the beast is a ghost (which couldn't be further from Simon's intent), chaos breaks loose. Ralph, having wrestled the conch away from Piggy and Jack, who are fighting over it, makes his next mistake by calling for a vote on who believes in ghosts. While Golding doesn't show us the tally of hands that go up, Ralph's reaction ("I see," p. 100) tells the story. The yelling match that ensues between Piggy, Jack, and Ralph shows the extent to which Piggy blames Jack for their situation, the extent to which Jack cannot abide hearing criticism from Piggy, and the extent to which Ralph is desperate for some kind of order. Jack's anger is also personal, linked to the jealousy he feels toward Ralph; a jealousy that he has nurtured since the first choosing of leader. Jack's comment, "You can't hunt, you can't sing" (p. 101), hearkens back to the authority he exercised as leader of the choir. And yet it is Jack who now wants to toss rules aside. Ralph tries to appeal to Jack's sense of order after Jack dismisses the rules: "Because the rules are the only thing we've got" (p. 101). Jack, feeling the new power granted by the boys' collective fear, returns to his theme of strength through hunting and almost seals the deal in his bid for power. "Bollocks to the rules! We're strong—we hunt! If there's a beast, we'll hunt it down! We'll close in and beat and beat and beat—!" (p. 101). As the assembly breaks apart, the scene shifts to the final coda on the chapter, featuring Ralph, Piggy, and Simon.

DISCUSSION/JOURNAL TOPIC: "BOLLOCKS TO THE RULES!"

What is the value in the rules that Ralph has set for the boys? Why does Jack reject them after he had agreed to them? What is the function of rules in general, and why do people break rules?

Although this final section of the chapter represents a settling down from the action of the assembly and its shouting and fighting, we cannot dismiss a few essential features. Ralph's refusal to blow the conch for fear the others will not respond, Piggy's explanation of why there cannot be ghosts, and Simon's reassurance of Ralph all figure into what will happen in later chapters. Perhaps most importantly, in this section we get a description from Piggy of real fear—that is, fear of the known, as compared to fear of the unknown. Piggy brings us into the psychology of the bullied, and while this is a touchy and difficult subject for some students to discuss, it may be worth taking class time to examine Piggy's statements at the bottom of page 103 and the top of page 104:

> "I'm scared of him," said Piggy, "and that's why I know him. If you're scared of someone you hate him but you can't stop thinking about him. You kid yourself he's all right really, an' then when you see him again; it's like asthma an' you can't breathe. I tell you what. He hates you too, Ralph—"
>
> "Me? Why me?"
>
> "I dunno. You got him over the fire; an' you're chief an' he isn't."
>
> "But he's, he's, Jack Merridew!"
>
> "I been in bed so much I done some thinking. I know about people. I know about me. And him. He can't hurt you: but if you stand out of the way he'd hurt the next thing. And that's me." (pp. 103–104)

It is at this point in the conversation that Simon reaffirms Ralph's right to the chieftainship. The boys have no answers to their problems, which leads to a reverie on the glory of the adult world. The boys believe in the adult process of negotiation, discussion, and peaceful resolution of conflict. The boys stand "in the darkness, striving unsuccessfully to convey the majesty of adult life" (p. 104). The irony of this statement is obvious if we remember how the boys got to the island in the first place, but if we have forgotten, we do not have to wait long for a reminder. Ralph's last words in the chapter call for a "message" from the adult world, a "sign or something" (p. 105), and as the next chapter begins, we once again see how Golding has crafted this story by giving the boys a sign, but not one that they can correctly interpret.

Six: Beast From Air

Although this is the start of a new chapter, we need to think of the first paragraph of Chapter 6 as continuing the scene that ends Chapter 5. There is no shift other than the turning of the page, until the boys go to sleep. Structurally, however, Chapter 6 is more closely tied to Chapter 7 than to Chapter 5, as both 6 and

7 treat one story, beginning with the fall of the parachutist early in Chapter 6 and continuing until Ralph and Jack see the dead man and run away at the end of Chapter 7. The same will be true of Chapters 8 and 9, which also present one story.

By this point in the novel, your students should have several threads of potential readings that they are pursuing. Some may be pursuing the power theme and thus may be tuned in to the ongoing struggle between Ralph and Jack. Some may be looking at a psychological reading, tracing the development of fear and irrational behavior. Others may be following the mistreatment of Piggy as the bullied outsider, and yet others may be pursuing Simon's character development. The beauty of *Lord of the Flies* is that it supports each of these readings and rewards close attention to details in the narrative, which is one of the reasons this book works well for teaching literary elements (see Chapter 5 of this book).

Chapter 6 of the novel may be divided into five distinct sections, which, as with all the chapters, may be further parsed. I prefer to see it as containing these particular sections:

1. The fall of the parachutist
2. Samneric see the "beast" at the fire
3. Samneric's report and discussion about a hunt for the beast
4. The trip to the Castle Rock (Ralph and Jack)
5. The boys on the Castle Rock

As mentioned above, the first paragraph of this chapter links the previous chapter and allows us to watch the conscientious biguns, Ralph and Simon, tending to the tortured Percival and then falling asleep. Next, Golding presents the lengthiest portrait in the book of the war being fought in the world outside the island, at "ten miles' [h]eight" (p. 106). Once again, we have a strong example of Golding's powers of description and control of narrative pace, as he shows us the dead parachutist falling to the island and then being blown in starts and fits upward by the wind before tangling in the trees and resting in a macabre position wherein each gust of wind causes the figure to go from a slouched over, head-down position to a sitting, upright position—perfect for frightening the youngsters. The "beast," as it will become known, sits like a marionette, waiting for the first child to encounter it.

From here, the scene shifts to Samneric at the fire. It is fitting that they are the first to see the beast, as they are excitable and already somewhat conflicted in their allegiances to Ralph. Note their conversation on page 108 about Ralph being "waxy" (i.e., crazy) about the fire. An ironic reading of the novel would require attention to this scene as an indicator that the boys are growing tired of Ralph's excessive exercise of authority. The reading is ironic in that most of the boys will trade Ralph's authority for Jack's, which is far more controlling. Samneric will be caught in the middle of that struggle later in the book.

The rest of this section is charming in a horror-film-like way because the boys, by experiencing their terror almost as one organism, allow us to feel their terror in an almost comical fashion. The scene shifts as they noiselessly run away.

The next section of the chapter shows yet another assembly, and it presents the same tropes we have seen with other assemblies: attempts at order from Ralph, provocation from Jack, fear and cynicism from Piggy followed by torments from Jack to Piggy, and an open struggle for power between Ralph and Jack. I see this scene as the beginning of the new regime of Jack, initiated by his open challenge to the primacy of the conch: "'Conch! Conch!' shouted Jack. 'We don't need the conch any more. We know who ought to say things. What good did Simon do speaking, or Bill, or Walter? It's time some people knew they've got to keep quiet and leave deciding things to the rest of us'" (p. 114). When Ralph tells him again to sit down, Jack refuses, and injects the one point that Ralph cannot refute: "This is a hunter's job" (p. 114).

DISCUSSION/JOURNAL TOPIC: LEADERSHIP CRISIS

We know more than the characters at this point because we know that the "beast" is just a dead parachutist. But imagine you were in the boys' position. Whose leadership would you embrace at that point? Who do you believe has the right to speak, and who does not? Is the conch necessary?

Certainly, the boys (except for Simon) seem to buy into Samneric's story of the beast, as they may all have already been ready to believe in the beast anyway, and we may interpret a twisted sort of relief for them to have their fears confirmed. With less doubt about it, they can take action, however absurd that action may be.

One other crucial detail to notice in this section of the chapter, something not one of the other characters (including Simon) notices, is Piggy's asthma attack. Very subtly, Golding's narrator shows Piggy holding his breath in the tension over Ralph and Jack's crisis of leadership, letting it out and then finding himself unable to take another breath. The "blue shadows creeping round his lips" (p. 115) indicate a very dangerous situation for anyone who knows the possibly fatal perils of an asthma attack, but "Nobody minded him" and they "left Piggy propped up on the platform" (p. 115). This could be taken to mean that they eventually did help him, but appears to mean that they just left him there. Ask students how that detail functions in their growing sense of the story.

The next section traces the boys' journey to the Castle Rock, where they logically believe the beast must live. The "theatrical caution" (p. 116) of Jack's pace shows us the farcical quality of this search. Simon senses the logical problem of a beast that, for all its horridness, cannot manage to run down Samneric.

Golding uses the term "inward sight" (p. 116) to describe Simon's perceptions, and I think the term fits well when we see how Simon's role in the story plays out later. Substituting for the beast a "picture of a human at once heroic and sick" (p. 116) may be a little too convenient an image for Golding to grant Simon, but it does elevate Simon to the status of a seer, even if the others cannot recognize it due to Simon's inability to speak persuasively. Ralph's perception of Simon is distorted as well because he cannot understand Simon, and as Simon runs into a tree and cuts his head open (in a classic gesture of the blind seer), Ralph only turns his thoughts inward. Shortly thereafter, as Jack and Ralph are discussing the likelihood that the beast is at the Castle Rock, Simon simply states that he doesn't believe in the beast, and Ralph responds "politely, as though agreeing about the weather. 'No. I suppose not'" (p. 118). This is a great moment because it offers the boys the opportunity to think logically about what they are doing—an opportunity they once again do not take.

This scene also gives us the first full description of the place that will later be the scene of Piggy's death. Your students may not be able to keep all the details straight (although by now they should be used to Golding's narrative style), but they should be able to pick up on the steepness of the place, the presence of the cave, and the many large rocks that seem to "totter" (p. 117). You will also want to point out the description of the table rock with the waves crashing over it, if only so they know it is there, as that is the same rock that Piggy will land on when he falls to his death.

Relating back to Simon's perception, there is a great moment of realization for Ralph (and we may choose to believe the other boys experience similar moments) when he comes to understand that he "did not really expect to meet any beast and didn't know what he would do about it if he did" (p. 119). This realization could save them if they stopped to analyze it. The whole enterprise is a serious kind of play. I use the word "play" because it will come up later in a crisis with Jack, but if we strip away the gravity of their situation, we can see this entire progression of actions as elaborate boys' play. They simply do not realize it, and Ralph does not verbalize his realization for the others to consider. As he and Jack stand at the top of the Castle Rock, Jack sees new opportunities for violent fun in the tottering rocks, and Ralph returns to his tired old theme of keeping a fire and getting rescued.

The final section of the chapter brilliantly displays the general disorder, with the boys finding a new play spot amidst their supposed danger, which "had faded with the darkness" (p. 121). But Ralph is not okay. He experiences a crisis of confidence that leads him to self-abuse, striking his knuckles against the rocks until he bleeds. The word "mutinously" (p. 122) is applied to the boys as they follow Ralph, the ultimate killjoy, who directs them to continue to the mountain to search for the beast and light the signal fire.

Seven: Shadows and Tall Trees

By this point in your class reading of the book, students can take on greater responsibility for completing their assigned reading without having to read together in class. A brisk combination of group and individual reading will allow you to make reading mode a topic of conversation. Ask whether they prefer the class reading or independent reading.

I divide Chapter 7 into four sections, as follows:

1. Ralph's state and his stress
2. The encounter with the boar and Ralph's reverie
3. The difficult climb toward the mountain
4. Ralph, Jack, and Roger climb the mountain to see the beast

As I mentioned earlier, this chapter is very closely tied to the previous chapter in that it continues the hunt for the beast originally seen by Samneric at the signal fire. But Golding first takes time to depict Ralph's realization of his perpetual filth ("the skin of the body, scurfy with brine," p. 124), which your students may not be able to relate to. Ask them to recall a time when they really needed a bath or shower but did not have access to one. Students can explore Ralph's state here, and discuss how Golding manipulates our allegiance to Ralph by allowing us to experience his interior thoughts to a greater extent than the other characters. As Ralph examines the expanse of ocean on the unprotected side of the island, he is filled with hopeless awe; a kind of existential stress. Simon's next humanitarian act—both recognizing and responding to Ralph's need—is one of the most touching moments in the book. There are not many moments of unsolicited kindness in this story, but this is one of them. Simon reassures Ralph, saying, "You'll get back to where you came from" (p. 125). What is both heartening and chilling about his statement, which he repeats for emphasis twice, is that he does not say "*We'll* get back to where *we* came from." As an examination of author's craft, a good way to approach this moment is to ask students how the long description of Ralph's physical state and his examination of the ocean sets us up for the moment together with Simon, and why Golding could not have just opened the chapter with that exchange. The smile they share is the last genuine smile in the book.

The second section of the chapter involves a diversion from their march to the mountain to hunt the beast, when pig droppings are discovered, not accidentally, by Roger. Roger has been in the background since his encounter with Henry in Chapter 3, and he reappears in this chapter to take on a larger role. Jack's "love" for the pig droppings (p. 126) suggests his decline into the filth represented by Beelzebub, Lord of the Flies. Jack and Roger will be tied together as chief and henchman soon. This chapter shows us a growing connection between the two. As Jack takes on leadership of the hunt for the beast, Ralph is free to daydream about home. This may be interpreted as a glance into Ralph's past to establish him as the book's everyman, but as his reverie of home is the only one described, his images of the safe, nurturing environment he sees in his memory stand for all the boys' memories of home, and we can assume that the other boys, at least occasionally, have similar fantasies. He is jarred out of the bucolic reminiscence by the shouting and tumult of a charging boar amongst the herd of boys.

The mayhem associated with the boar leads to another battle between Ralph and Jack for the boys' respect. Ralph shows his vulnerability to the life Jack espouses by his reaction to hitting the boar in the snout. Hunting was "good after all" (p. 128), but Jack cannot let Ralph have his moment as the hunter. He quickly berates Ralph for letting the boar get away and sports his own wound to regain the other boys' favor. What your students may notice in this scene is how predictable the characters are, including Simon, who tells Jack that he is wounded and should suck his wound, something Jack is willing to do. Even Ralph, who shows a new dimension, is predictable in his desire to be liked by the boys.

DISCUSSION/JOURNAL TOPIC: DO RALPH'S ACTIONS SURPRISE YOU?

Ask students to consider the following questions: What in this scene surprises you about Ralph's behavior, and what makes sense to you? Are you surprised when he joins in the sport, jabbing Robert, and then gets carried away in the emotion of the moment? Is it Ralph who screams "Kill him! Kill him!" when Robert acts the role of the pig? Ask students to discuss the ensuing play that gets out of hand, leading to Robert's terror, and the dialogue that follows it about how to make the "game" better.

The shift to the next section of the chapter is sudden and stark, as Ralph, who has just been carried away with the violent play-acting, sits up and redirects the boys back to their pursuit of the beast on the mountain. His obsession with the fire leads him to make another bad decision: to go up to the fire and relight it. Golding's narrator, never far removed from the physical characteristics of the island, returns to close examination of the treacherous path the boys travel and the futility of their attempts to reach the mountain by the route Ralph has chosen for them. The tension between Ralph and Jack is foregrounded in this section, as is Simon's uncanny ability to surprise everyone with his bravery. Any student who is primarily interested in the conflict between Ralph and Jack will find plenty of material for analysis here, as their bickering becomes almost tedious, with the two continually challenging each other until Ralph breaks the expected norms and asks Jack, "Why do you hate me?" (p. 134). Ask your students why the other boys react as though Ralph has said something indecent. Do students think that detail is tied to the time period when the book was written or would kids react the same way today to such an open question? The complicated emotions of the two characters both repel and attract the other boys. What may be lost in the reading of this scene is how the personal animosity between Ralph and Jack is leading them to make bad decisions, the greatest of which is the foolishness of going up the mountain in the dark. It is only due to this plot development, however, that the rest of the book can play out as it does, for they would no doubt recognize the dead parachutist for what he is if they were to wait until morning to ascend the mountain.

The three boys who make the ascent get to experience the residue of their first bad decision when they try to go through the burnt-out area below the mountain, where their first fire had been lit. They could be treading through the "devils of dust" (p. 136) that used to be a young boy with a mulberry-colored birthmark. The disorientation they experience, the darkness, the struggle, and the exhaustion, together with the tired and continually snarky comments between Ralph and Jack, prepare them mentally for the drastic and tragic misinterpretation of what they find when they get to the top.

There's an odd moment on page 137 after Jack one-ups Ralph and steals forward to the fire site. Ralph is left together with Roger, who does not speak and who is described as "impervious." Ralph can't interpret Roger, he can't figure out Jack, and he, most tragically, can't recognize the dead parachutist, perhaps because it is dark, or perhaps because, having "fused his fear and loathing into a hatred" (p. 140), he cannot see anything clearly. The chapter ends with three frightened little boys running away from a grisly set of human remains.

As is often the case in tragic stories, the difference between disaster and a less calamitous outcome hinges on a simple misperception, aided by the willingness of the characters to accept their misperceptions. In Shakespeare's *Othello*, for example, the Moor believes what he sees to be evidence of his wife's infidelity simply because Iago suggests it, and because his jealous mind wants to believe it. In *Lord of the Flies*, a simple questioning of their perception would lead the boys to reexamine what they saw on the mountaintop—but only Simon will have the courage to do so, albeit with disastrous results.

Eight: Gift for the Darkness

Just as Chapters 6 and 7 represent one episode that concerns itself with the hunting and discovery of the beast, so too are Chapters 8 and 9 closely linked, relating one episode. The episode opens with the next morning's cruel dawn, which follows Ralph, Jack, and Roger's supposed sighting of the beast, and ends with Simon's murder. To respect Golding's chapter breaks, I will discuss the chapters separately, with the acknowledgment that they can be treated in the classroom as a single unit. Chapter 8 may be divided into the following sections:

1. The assembly and separation of Jack
2. The assembly following Jack's departure
3. Building the fire on the beach; the biguns defect
4. Simon goes to his place
5. The killing of the sow
6. Simon and the Lord of the Flies
7. Ralph and Piggy and the first attack by Jack's group
8. A second assembly with the remaining boys
9. A return to Simon with the Lord of the Flies

This list is long, though Sections 4, 6, and 9 are all the same scene. Golding uses a cut-away strategy to shift us from one scene to another and then back, something that has not occurred thus far in the book. The technique is necessary for the dramatic effect of speeding up time. As the boys are splintering off into groups, Golding allows us to witness concurrent activities using techniques similar to what movie or television crews use. This may be another good chapter to jigsaw in discussion.

The first section begins with Piggy, who is miserable, doubting Ralph and asking him for the nth time whether he is sure that the beast is real. Everything has changed with the certainty that what was unthinkable to the most rational of the boys is real. Ralph's willingness to believe in the existence of the beast, having imperfectly seen it in the darkness of the night before, creates an atmosphere of despair in which anything bad can happen. It is important in the opening of the scene that Jack is present and that Simon appears (we may assume that he has slept again in his secret bower). Ralph's resignation and admission, "We're beaten" (p. 142), leads Jack to raise the question, "What about my hunters?" (p. 142). Ralph's responding insult, "Boys armed with sticks" (p. 142), sets off a chain of events that results in the splintering of the group. Piggy recognizes Ralph's blunder right away, as he is keenly aware of Jack at all times.

By this point in the story, all the personalities of the major characters are well developed, and we can see their further actions as extensions of the character portraits we have drawn in our interpretations (see SAS #8: Character Charts).

Jack calls an assembly—his first act of rebellion. Ralph's challenge to Jack's authority to call a meeting is half-hearted and short-lived, and having taken the conch from Jack, he hands it back in frustration. "Oh, take it! Go on—talk!" he says (p. 143). Jack, perhaps sensing an opportunity, addresses the possibility of the beast and what it can or cannot do; then, instead of proposing a solution or plan of action, he attacks Ralph. It is a question of interpretation in this scene as to whether Jack simply sees an opportunity to seize power, or whether he is childishly upset at Ralph's earlier insult of the hunters. Either way, he makes his play for leadership and fails, at least in the short run.

A couple of things to notice here (and this is another great scene to act out in class) are Jack's appeal to the social structure of their previous lives—"He isn't a prefect and we don't know anything about him" (p. 144)—and the intensity of Jack's emotions. Jack wants power, but it may be that he truly believes that Ralph is a poor leader and that he can do a better job. Absent his bullying of Piggy, it is possible that he could make a legitimate claim on leadership, but he has misinterpreted his crowd . . . or has he? Another significant comment to notice is Jack's line when he decides to leave: "I'm not going to play any longer. Not with you" (p. 145). This line allows Golding to remind us that they are boys, not adults. If Jack sees it as play—even if it's a deeply intense game—then he can throw the "fun" of hunting at his audience, which has rejected him for the time being. This may be his most effective line, as the boys will soon find out that Ralph, with his authority and his single-minded focus on rescue, is not as fun to be around as Jack is. The section ends with Jack disappearing into the forest.

The second section of the chapter is short, but contains two significant events. The first is Piggy's reassertion of himself into the mix in Jack's absence. In Ralph's despair, however, Ralph ignores him, saying "There's no help, Piggy. Nothing to be done" (p. 146). Piggy is momentarily silenced, which gives Simon the opportunity to suggest the only rational thing possible, which is to climb the mountain. This is an interesting scene to discuss with students in light of the old connection between the message and the messenger. When Simon suggests that they climb the mountain, he is roundly rejected. None of the other boys even dignifies his suggestion with a response. But if Ralph had suggested the same thing, it may have been interpreted as bravery and leadership. Simon's symbolic positioning of himself "as far away from the others as possible" (p. 147) continues the process of his alienation that leads eventually to his unfortunate death. Piggy's brilliant (or perhaps simply obvious) idea to build a fire on the beach overshadows Simon's suggestion, which could save them from their further descent into savagery.

A narrative shift occurs as the boys begin to build the fire, and the next section of the chapter shows the narrator summarizing the scene of purposeful fire building, focusing on Piggy's righteous dismissal of Jack and his expanding liberty. This fire building parallels the first, disastrous fire that they had built in Chapter 2. One noticeable detail is the narrator's description of "panic in the energy and hysteria in the cheerfulness" (p. 148), which indicates a subtext that contradicts the boys' behavior on the surface. It does not take long for Ralph and the others to notice that most of the biguns have abandoned them. Students may want to discuss why this flight of the biguns occurs. You may pose it to them as a choice between possible causes: the lure of the hunt, the drudgery of keeping a fire going, or the annoyance of following Piggy as Ralph's right-hand man. Students may offer other reasons for the boys' defections to what will become known as Jack's tribe. For his part, Piggy could not be happier, as he appears to be safe, at least for the time being. The beast is nothing to Piggy. His beast is Jack Merridew, a known menace. This section ends with the acknowledgment that Simon is also missing. While Ralph is surprised by his absence, neither Ralph nor Piggy entertains the notion that Simon would join the others. Ralph's suggestion that Simon may have climbed the mountain is important for at least two reasons, the first being that neither boy considers going after him and the second being that it is only they who should know that, when the "beast" comes out of the forest at the calamitous conclusion to Chapter 9, it is only Simon.

The next section of the chapter shows us Simon stealing into his secret place, to suffer in the heat. This small portrait is almost bizarre, as Simon, seeming to purposefully suffer, sits without water and grows "very thirsty" as the "arrows" of the sun beat down on him (p. 151). This small portrait, reminiscent of Christ in the desert or perhaps in the garden of Gethsemane, serves as prelude to Simon's hallucinogenic encounter with the pig's head.

The next section of the chapter shows Jack in full renaissance, with a following and no contestation of his right to be chief. Golding reminds us of their descent by having the narrator recount that the boys wearing the remains of their choir hats had once had voices that were "the song of angels" (p. 151). The next line following this description is Jack's assertion "We'll hunt. I'm going to be chief" (p. 151). He then goes on to dismiss the beast by saying that they won't "bother about" it (p. 152). This scene illustrates Jack's authoritative style—in case we had forgotten it from Chapter 1—and it demonstrates his plan to "get more of the biguns away from the conch and all that" (p. 152). His idea to offer a tribute offering to the beast can be taken a couple of ways. Your students may just read that as a great boyish idea, part of the adventure of living on a mysterious island, or they may see it as Jack's calculating power narrative. In other words, does Jack really believe in the beast? What did he see up on the mountain? Ask your students whether they think that Jack believes in the beast.

Activity (SAS #15): Who Believes in the Beast?

Have students fill in the chart on SAS #15, indicating different characters' attitudes toward "the beast." Have them write notes on what each character thinks about the beast, and indicate any changes in the characters' attitude or beliefs that take place as the story progresses.

What follows Jack's little meeting is one of the most famous and graphic scenes in the book: the gang-rape killing of the sow. You will note the descriptions of the sow lying in "deep maternal bliss" (p. 154) with her littluns, and the violence with which the boys attack and kill her, which many critics have astutely pointed out is told in sexual terms: "wedded to her in lust," "excited by the long chase," "heavy and fulfilled upon her," and so on (p. 154).

I hope you will feel comfortable discussing this scene with your students and that you will get to the point in the conversation where you ask them why Golding would choose to represent these prepubescent boys gang-raping an animal, then bragging about it in crude terms. You may notice changes in the other boys following this scene, as the taboo against violence that Jack has already overcome fades away from them all (even Henry, the littlun!). We also get the first image of a stick sharpened at both ends, something Roger creates for Jack, which establishes him as Jack's dark assistant. Jack's act of cutting off the sow's head and impaling it on a stick, then leaving the stick for the beast, demonstrates the extent of his savagery and aligns him with Mr. Kurtz in Conrad's *Heart of Darkness*. Perhaps because he comes from a highly strict, oppressive environment in the choir, Jack easily establishes a new authoritarian regime, as ceremony and ritual are natural to him.

A couple of plausibility issues occur here, too. One is Jack's ability to cut off the head with his knife, apparently right through what would be a considerable set of vertebrae. The other possible stretch of plausibility here is that Maurice and Robert are able to skewer the carcass and carry it. If it really was a large sow, perhaps a couple hundred pounds, it would be quite difficult for two kids to haul. If any students point these issues out, rather than dismissing their lack of ability to suspend disbelief, you may consider congratulating them for close reading. Also note that, although Jack's group seems to be more comfortable in their surroundings than Ralph and Piggy's group (with their barely suppressed panic and hysteria), they all run away "as fast as they could" (p. 156) toward the beach, leaving their offering for the beast.

The next section, the first part of Simon's encounter with the Lord of the Flies, starts with our recognition that he has witnessed the murder of the sow. If your students are attracted to Simon, and many of them will be, they may be emotionally moved by this recognition and the scene that follows. Golding's narrator allows us to experience Simon's fade toward hallucination by suggesting a voice in his head admonishing him for his difference and his understanding. This interior dialogue is matched with external description of the scene, the guts, the flies, and the butterflies' abandonment of the space (which your students may note as symbolic). Also mentioned is the slow development of what will be a violent storm. You can have a student trace the first mention of the changing weather and analyze how Golding returns to it like a leitmotif, building it as the shifting scenes in the chapter reach their crescendo. As the "pulse" begins to beat on Simon's right temple, the scene shifts back to Ralph and Piggy.

At this point, Ralph and Piggy have reached a new low. They cannot keep a fire going, they complain about the remaining friends they have, and they have no plan. Their conversation is at once lame and heartbreaking. Ralph wants Piggy to explain to him why "things break up like they do" (p. 159). We see Ralph's essential problem: his inability to "think like a grownup," which is ironic, given that he thinks very much like a grownup, but with a child's limitations. Piggy's response is characteristically British, paraphrasing the official motto of the London people during the Blitz: "We just got to go on, that's all" (p. 159). As Piggy takes the opportunity to blame Jack, Jack himself appears beneath the disguise of his war paint. With two others, he steals a burning branch and invites his enemies to the coming feast. The thunderclouds boom, and Jack requires his two assistants to chant "The Chief has spoken" (p. 161) as a message to Ralph, indicating that if he has any doubts about who is in charge of the splinter group, he should get over them. Jack's inviting them to the feast is a brilliant move, as it puts Ralph and Piggy in a position of being beholden to Jack. But it is also brilliant in that it drives a little wedge between Ralph and Piggy, with Ralph dismissing Piggy, returning to his popular refrain: "Sucks to your ass-mar" (p. 161).

From here the scene shifts to the most pathetic assembly of the book. Ralph is increasingly unable to think, and thus unable to lead. Everyone is attracted to the romance of hunting and the hunger for meat. The storm continues to build. Bill's short speech on the bottom of page 162 turns the tide, and they all implicitly give in to their desire to join the fun at Jack's party.

The final section of this chapter returns us to Simon and sets us up for Chapter 9. By this time (if we can imagine the amount of time has passed that would allow for the events of the previous section to happen), the voice inside Simon's head has burst into audibility, as Golding signifies through the presence of quotation marks around the comments of the Lord of the Flies. I think it is very important for the students to experience this scene on their own terms and discuss it as they see fit, without insisting that they parse out every single exchange. It is a mystical scene, and to reduce it to a single meaning during a first read-through is not going to be a good investment in time. On the other hand, if students want to get a good solid reading, let them run with it. One thing they may not notice is that the voice of the Lord of the Flies, having called Simon a "silly little boy" (p. 163), asks rhetorically whether Simon likes Ralph, but he also includes Piggy and Jack. The inclusion of Jack is important here, as it implies that Simon loves all of them, even Jack. Note that Simon knows that he's hallucinating: "Pig's head on a stick," he says (p. 164). He knows he's on the verge of fainting, feeling "one of his times coming on" (p. 164). As he approaches unconsciousness, the voice threatens him, not only foreshadowing what will come in the next chapter, but hearkening back to the theme of child violence against those who are different.

Nine: A View to a Death

This chapter is difficult to absorb, as it presents one of the most iconic scenes of violence in 20th-century literature. As mentioned above, Chapter 9 is really a continuation of Chapter 8, and it is as though Golding needed to parse out the chapters in order to give the reader a breather before unleashing the momentous climax to the storm, the conflicts of personalities, the misperceptions, and the ritualistic violence.

The chapter falls into the following sections:

1. Simon awakens and heads to the mountain, discovering the parachutist
2. Ralph and Piggy consider their options
3. The feast and the killing of Simon
4. The illumination of Simon's body

The first section again demonstrates the careful pace of the narrative, with deep description of Simon's unconscious body and the gathering storm. Students may discuss why Golding takes his time with this particular image of Simon beneath the hanging pig's head, and the care with which he describes his blood vessel bursting, the blood, the flies, Simon's dazed awakening, and his resolution to go on with the line, "What else is there to do?" (p. 167). Simon is here repeating himself from the scene in the last chapter when he suggested they climb the mountain to confront the beast. Simon takes on the burden of the entire group, a burden that he will be unable to lift from them, even though he will eventually free the parachutist. Students may notice that the narrator continues the careful description of the landscape features, the creepers that impede Simon's progress, and the deep jungle flora. Golding never lets us forget that these boys are physically struggling against nature throughout the book.

DISCUSSION/JOURNAL TOPIC: SIMON

Students may want to talk about Simon's character traits here, as he completes his penultimate act of charity by freeing the dead man and prepares for his final act of charity, which will lead to his violent death. What do they think of this boy? Ask them to pick details in the descriptions of Simon in this scene that define him for them. Eventually, they may wish to discuss or write about what Simon symbolizes, how he parallels Jesus Christ, or how he serves as an inadequate spiritual guide for the group. Perhaps he may be likened to a tragic hero (as may Ralph or Piggy). Even stripping symbolism or metaphor away from this scene, we are left with the extraordinary act of freeing the dead man, despite the physical revulsion (and convulsion!) it causes Simon. Perhaps a more powerful investigation would be to ask your students whether they know anyone among their peer group who exhibits the charitable traits of Simon, or better yet, whether they see (or would like to see) these traits in themselves.

ACTIVITY (SAS #16): PLATO'S "ALLEGORY OF THE CAVE"

Another way to look at Simon is as the hypothetical figure in Plato's "Allegory of the Cave" who is released from bondage and permitted to see the truth. Access any print or online version of the allegory and have students read. (As of printing, this reading can be found at http://www.historyguide.org/intellect/allegory.html.) Have them construct parallels between the figure in the allegory who is permitted to leave the cave and see the truth and how he would surely be killed by the others if he were to return to the cave and tell them what is real. A two-column journal will serve to organize the parallels.

The first section of the chapter ends with Simon, face bloodied and staggering, going to reveal his secret to the other boys.

The second section of the chapter presents a little scene with Ralph and Piggy, and there are good details here to note, even though the scene is only a little more than a page in length. First, we have the continued teasing of Piggy by Ralph, who is Piggy's ally, and Piggy's response. When Ralph squirts water at Piggy, "expecting him to retire meekly as usual and in pained silence," Piggy beats water in Ralph's face and shouts "Stop it!" (p. 169). This is a reminder that Ralph has never given up his role as a bully, even if he is not a fierce one like Jack is. What is subtle here is Ralph's surprise at Piggy's exasperation. It is as though Ralph believes that Piggy accepts his role as victim, perhaps even relishing it. It never occurs to Ralph that Piggy might not like being messed with.

Another element of this scene to notice is the connection between the brewing storm and the tension in the boys. The littluns at the pool are "trying to extract comfort from a wetness warmer than blood" (p. 169), and Piggy has a pain in his head. We have parallel quotes from Ralph and Piggy that reveal their states of mind:

> Ralph: "I wish the rain would come."
> Piggy: "I wish we could go home." (p. 169)

Ralph may want the rain to come so that the other boys will contritely return to the shelters, or he may want the tension of the storm buildup to end. Piggy seems to sense that matters are worsening and that he is personally threatened. When they notice that Samneric, Bill, and the littluns have gone, they have a very short exchange before they, too, decide to join Jack's party, even if they do so disapprovingly. Your class may discuss why Ralph and Piggy attend the feast. Is the lure of meat just that powerful? In other words, is this a story about the human need to be carnivores? Are they, as Piggy suggests, just trying "to make sure nothing happens" (p. 170)? Or is it the pull of the fun of playing pretend savages that they cannot resist? Either way, when they get to the party, what they find will not be exactly what they expected. You may remind your students that now everyone is together except for Simon.

The third section of the chapter presents Jack, "painted and garlanded," sitting on a log "like an idol" (p. 170). If this is "play," it's a fun game for Jack, as he gets to be treated like a god. The boys are "laughing, singing, lying, squatting, or standing on the grass, holding food in their hands" (p. 170). Apparently, despite the gathering storm, they feel safe and happy. Treating Jack as a god appears to be a small price to pay for such fun. Ralph and Piggy act strangely in this scene, pretending not to be a part of the group. This is a scene that, even if your students read it at home as homework, should be reread out loud in class, to capture the dramatic intensity and to try to make sense of how the combination of the fire, the meat, the dialogue between Jack and Ralph, the storm, and the dance all contribute to the frenzy that will lead to Simon's death. The scene may be broken into three subsections, the first being the description of the party and Jack's offering of meat to Ralph and Piggy. Ralph and Piggy's faked nonchalance as they stand outside the group is sadly overcome when two boys bump into Piggy and scald him with burning grease. In our consideration of Ralph, we must note that when Piggy is burned, Ralph and the others "were united and relieved by a storm of laughter. Piggy once more was the center of social derision so that everyone felt cheerful and normal" (p. 171). What about Piggy? Given his behavior toward Ralph in the scene before, how would we expect him to feel?

Jack takes the perfect opportunity to show largesse and solidify his practical power by commanding one of his nameless servants to "Take them some meat" (p. 171). Ask your students what the implications are of Ralph and Piggy accepting the meat and eating it, "dribbling" (p. 171). Some have likened the meat to a kind of spiritual poison of forbidden fruit (Olsen, 2000). But Jack demonstrates the extent of his drive for power by threatening implicitly while the boys eat. Ralph is reduced to looking uneasily at the fire and moving away, like a pack dog that has been replaced as the alpha. Piggy, "betrayed by his stomach," (p. 171), makes a move for more meat than has been offered, and thus sets the stage for Jack's threatening gestures. Jack takes pains to demonstrate how far the other boys are willing to go in serving him. Henry, the stout littlun, is now in the service of his chief, bringing him water. One of the more famous lines in the book follows, a description of the painted idol, Jack: "Power lay in the brown swell of his forearms: authority sat on his shoulder and chattered in his ear like an ape" (p. 172). Ask students what this line might mean, and also ask them to recall any other references in the book to "apes" and how they may be connected.

DISCUSSION/JOURNAL TOPIC: THE STORM

Throughout this scene, as has been developed during the chapter, is the building storm. Ask your students what warnings are given in the description of the evening and the storm, some of them more obvious than others. They may explore other works they have read that featured pivotal storms. Is the storm symbolic in *Lord of the Flies*?

For his part, Ralph seems unable to understand the extent to which he has diminished in the eyes of the hunters (and perhaps the others). His invocation of the election, the rescue fire, and the conch all prove ineffective against Jack's strength and the power of "fun" accentuated by the nearer and more threatening lightning strikes. Piggy seems to understand and tries to pull Ralph away from the gathering, sensing trouble. But Ralph makes one last point that seems to lead to a crisis. It is obvious that torrential rain will come, and Ralph mentions the shelters. As the boys, including the hunters, seem to realize for the first time that nature is about to slam them, Jack does what has been done repeatedly when chaos starts to erupt: He causes a distraction. "Do our dance!" he shouts. "Come on! Dance!" (p. 174).

The passages that follow describe the dance, the explosion of the storm, and Simon's unfortunate timing in breaking upon the scene at exactly the wrong time. To follow up on the behavior of Ralph and Piggy, we see that "under the threat of the sky" (p. 174) they join in to the mock killing easily. Roger first mimics the pig, and it is also of note that these children are armed with spears, hot spits, and clubs. This can no longer be described as a picnic. As students work through this scene, have them identify narrative shifts between description of the storm, description of the dance, repetition of the chant, and description of Simon, alternately referred to by name and as "the beast" (p. 175). They may need to piece it out in order to understand what happens. It will be good to address the mention of Simon's name, and the specificity of what is said. Ask students to interpret whether the mention of his name means that only Ralph, or perhaps Ralph and Piggy, recognize who it is, or whether all the boys at some point recognize that it is Simon. Our interpretation of their actions will be affected by our sense of their cognizance of the beast being Simon. We can also ask why Ralph and Piggy do not struggle to help Simon instead of participating in the murder.

DISCUSSION/JOURNAL TOPIC: MOB MENTALITY

Have students look back at scenes involving play violence, starting with the first circle that mimicked killing a pig. How has their play transformed to mob violence, and why has that happened?

As the scene reaches its climax and subsides, and the boys notice how small the beast is, we wonder how much realization they have before the storm breaks. Almost like a parodic reversal of the deus ex machina, the dead parachutist is raised by the storm and floats down, swooping over the boys and driving them running and screaming into the forest. Golding here will not allow the boys a revelation even after their darkest deeds. The parachutist is swept out to sea, and they will not be able to discover the truth that Simon offered them. Like Plato's chained figures in the cave, they are doomed to see a reality that is just shadows dancing against flames.

The final section of this chapter is the beautifully sad description of the transformation (or transubstantiation) of Simon's body, reclaimed lovingly by nature in the form of tiny sea creatures. The reference to the pull of the sun and moon on the Earth as participating in this change, this reclamation, connects Simon with the natural world in a way that separates him from the others.

ACTIVITY (SAS #17): MOVIE MADNESS

In the Peter Brook movie version of *Lord of the Flies* (1963), the scene of Simon's body floating in the water is beautifully done, with the sound of a boys' choir singing "Kyrie Eleison" (Lord, Have Mercy) in the background. Have students view the movie version of Simon's death from the 1963 film, then write what effects the elements of the scene have on them. Have them consider the soundtrack, the images, the dialogue, and the movement. Then watch the same scene from the 1990 film version (dir. Harry Hook), and have students repeat the exercise. As a class, discuss these cinematic representations of the scene.

I want to acknowledge that sensitive readers will find this to be a difficult scene to read and to reread, and you may have some students who react emotionally to this. If you do, that's not a bad thing, as it will demonstrate the extent to which they are invested in the story. They may also be upset that it is so bleak, and that what may be the most attractive or interesting character should meet such an end. Your willingness to entertain discussion of the emotional impact of Simon's death may lead to good discussion. You may also ask your students to predict what impact Simon's killing will have on the other characters before reading Chapter 10.

Ten: The Shell and the Glasses

Chapter 10 is a short chapter that moves quickly, consisting primarily of dialogue with short descriptions of the boys and their movements. Absent from this chapter are long descriptive passages related to the natural setting or the weather. I divide the chapter into the following sections, which I will discuss below:

1. Piggy and Ralph rediscover one another and Samneric
2. Roger and Robert at the entrance to the Castle Rock
3. Jack and the tribe in the cave
4. Ralph, Piggy, and Samneric argue over the fire
5. Ralph, Piggy, and Samneric try to sleep
6. The attack on the shelter from Jack, Roger, and Maurice

While Jack and his tribe, especially Roger, give us the vision of descent into savagery in this book, it is Ralph and Piggy who demonstrate the tendency in our natures to rationalize, to dismiss, to excuse our wrongdoings. In the first section of the chapter, we see Ralph physically beaten, ostensibly as a result of the dance and murder of Simon. He is sporting a swollen cheek and a large scab on his knee. Ralph's hair is no longer described as fair; rather, it is just "yellow" (p. 178). The conch is described as "fragile" (p. 178) and Ralph symbolically sits facing the chief's seat, rather than on it. He immediately brings up Simon's name to Piggy. They sit with "befouled bodies" (p. 179) and open the conversation that will move from Ralph's exclamation that they murdered Simon to, in only a few pages, a shared assertion by Ralph, Piggy, and Samneric that they were not part of the group, that they left early, that they did not participate in the murder. What we may piece together from the conversation is that perhaps Piggy is the only one who did not physically have a hand in Simon's death, but the guilt is too much for Ralph to process, and he appears to be losing his grip on sanity. Piggy, perhaps realizing what is at stake, can't have Ralph blaming himself, and so starts the process of rationalization.

One thing that stands out here is Ralph's admission that he was not scared (p. 180). Piggy refuses to believe it was murder, and the first indication that he is convincing Ralph is when Ralph says, "You were outside. Outside the circle. You never really came in. Didn't you see what we—what they did?" (p. 180). That shift from what *we* did to what *they* did marks Ralph's first step outside of taking responsibility for his part in the killing. Shortly after, he says, "You didn't see what they did" (p. 181). Piggy, for his part, uses high emotion—his voice almost squeaking, like a pig's—to bring sense to Ralph, claiming at one point that Simon brought the killing on himself: "He asked for it" (p. 181). Although it was Piggy who mentioned in the previous chapter that he wanted to go home, Ralph says it emphatically in this chapter, and he admits that he is frightened. He doesn't say that he is frightened of Jack or that he is frightened of the hunters. He says, "I'm frightened. Of us" (p. 181).

We see the remains of their society: just the four directionless boys, unable to admit to their savagery. The twins, by their own words, were not even there, and by the end of this section they have all convinced themselves that they were not at the murder.

The next sections of the chapter show the dynamics of Jack's tribe following the murder of Simon. While this part of the chapter reads as one scene, I like to split it into three parts. The first part consists of Roger and Robert outside the cave at the Castle Rock. The narrator places in Roger's conscience phrases like "terrible night" and "horrors of the island" (p. 182), which indicate that fear has been a factor for Roger. An important detail to notice here is that Robert introduces the mechanism of the log jammed under one of the large rocks at the top of the cliff. Also note that Roger sees through the nonsense of having to identify himself to Robert, identification being one of Jack's rituals. Nevertheless, Roger approves of the new regime, and, like Goebbels to Jack's Hitler, says of Jack: "He's a proper chief, isn't he?" (p. 183)

The next line, spoken after an indication that both boys remember the night before, comes when Robert says: "He's going to beat Wilfred" (p. 183). Robert's giggling while describing Wilfred's forced bondage and impending corporal punishment indicates that the boys have in some way been liberated by the violent dance of the night before. Here, the narrator focuses on Roger, processing the news of Jack's growing reign of terror, "assimilating the possibilities of irresponsible authority" (p. 184). This passage recalls Roger's earlier exhilaration when throwing rocks at Henry (see Chapter 4 in the book). The taboo against hitting his target has been removed, and Roger appears eager to test out his new perspective.

The scene shifts to the cave, where the chief sits. Details your students should notice include the fact that Jack's face is painted, that the tribe lays "before him" like worshippers, and that he is never once referred to as "Jack" by the narrator. He is only "the chief." His tongue is "a triangle of startling pink" (p. 184) as he speaks, and he perpetuates the myth of the beast to increase his control. Jack has become a skilled fearmonger.

DISCUSSION/JOURNAL TOPIC: THE TRIBE AND THE BEAST

What is the beast? Look at the section on pages 184–185. How is Jack able to perpetuate the myth of the beast? Look at the dialogue and the narrator's descriptions of the boys' reactions to what is said. What skill does Jack show here, and how does he manage to be persuasive? How does the mask of paint help him achieve his goals?

When Bill, the latest of the defectors to Jack's tribe, asks how they will light fire, Jack sees an opportunity to humiliate and harm Piggy again. It is not by accident that Roger accompanies Jack to steal fire, and Maurice volunteers also, although he mentions the possibility of meeting the beast on their way to steal fire.

It is clear that all of the boys are disoriented by the previous night's events—all except for Jack, who appears to have gained a kind of terrible clarity. He suggests the incantation of the dance as a defense against the beast.

The next section of the chapter presents the argument about labor and the fire between Samneric and Ralph, while Piggy stands by. The scene starts, however, with the boys gathering wood, and Ralph tacitly admitting his fear of going without fire in the night. As the boys imagine dramatic salvation by making a boat or a radio or a plane, Ralph makes the only real contemporary reference in the book, by imagining that they could be taken prisoner by "the Reds" (p. 187). Although the book often feels like it is set against a World War II background, it was published during the Cold War. Golding was very careful not to tie the book to contemporary cultural references, but the "Reds" is a reference to the Communist Soviet Union—this is perhaps Golding's only slip in that regard.

After Eric suggests that capture by the Reds would be better than being taken by Jack's tribe, Ralph makes a shocking statement about Simon, that he "said something about a dead man" (p. 187), and it is indicated through the narration that Ralph understood that he had seen a figure in a parachute. It's as though Ralph is close to piecing together the truth that Simon had tried to deliver. But Ralph is too self-conscious to examine it closely with the other boys, so he instead changes the subject. This leads to the argument about fire. Students will recognize in this scene repetition of earlier tropes: Piggy's unwillingness (or inability) to do physical labor, Ralph's inability to hold the thought of rescue in his mind for any length of time, and their collective inability to keep the fire going. Once Ralph gives up on the fire, they go to the shelters to sleep.

The boys settle into the shelter, and this is the first look we have of their actual routine of settling into sleep. Ralph daydreams of home as the boys, somewhat innocently, try to come to rest. They even joke about going crazy if they are not rescued, though it lacks humor. Ralph teases Piggy (but in a less harmful way than before) about sending his auntie a letter. This section eases right into the next as Ralph falls asleep, but is shaken awake by Piggy in the next line.

The final section of the chapter is the attack on the shelter by Jack, Roger, and Maurice. This scene marks a significant change in the reality of the island. While Jack before sought to separate himself from Ralph's group, he now is actively antagonistic: in essence, declaring war. He needs a resource—Piggy's glasses—and so, instead of asking for them, he attacks and takes them. The violence done to Piggy in the past was sanctioned by the boys' shared code of domination by bullies over the weak and different. Now, Ralph—Jack's former, tentative friend—is included as an enemy. The violence done in the murder of Simon could be attributed to the frenzy of the dance, the storm, or mere misperception and fear of the beast. This attack, on the other hand, is premeditated, calculated, and executed according to a plan. As such, the world has changed for these boys.

Several details in the narration of the attack may slip by first-time readers, but ask your students what they notice when they read this section. Some may notice that Ralph still believes in the beast, as he "desperately" prays that the beast "would prefer littluns" (p. 192). That is an extraordinary statement about Ralph's character, and an indictment of his ability to lead. Some students may notice Piggy's impending asthma attack. Some may notice the similarities in the description of Ralph's fight and Eric's story of what happened to him. Almost comically, they must have been fighting each other. Once again, the boys find themselves at a new low. Piggy cannot see and Ralph cannot lead. As such, Samneric, the last two biguns in Ralph and Piggy's group, are vulnerable.

A small coda to the chapter shows "three figures" (including "the chief") happily (if nervously) returning to their camp (p. 194). The attack solidifies Jack's power: "He was a chief now in truth" (p. 194). One other detail that Golding introduces with effect is the boys turning cartwheels "down by the moving streak of phosphorescence" (p. 194). This is presumably the same phosphorescence that had decorated Simon's dead body, so the image of the exultant savages turning cartwheels indicates their lack of remorse over what had occurred only one night before.

Eleven: Castle Rock

This chapter represents the culmination of the society of the boys on the island, and the end of the arguments between Ralph and Jack. Like the murder of Simon, the killing of Piggy is an iconic scene in the book. If your students have engaged with the novel and the story at this point, they may read straight through to the end of the book, even if you only assign this chapter. It is difficult to stop reading between Chapters 11 and 12. I have been dividing these chapters to facilitate discussions. This chapter, however, only has two sections (though the second section has several movements in it). I resist breaking apart the confrontation at the Castle Rock into separate sections because it moves with breathtaking pace toward the end. Part of this is Golding's brilliance: Having controlled his pace so carefully throughout, he unleashes this rapid scene so that we are left in shock as Piggy's body is washed to sea and Ralph is forced to flee in terror. So let us go slowly and work through it together. The chapter falls into these two sections:

1. The assembly on the platform
2. The confrontation at the Castle Rock

The first section of the chapter describes the preconfrontation assembly down on the platform. Ralph and the twins are noticeably beaten up. Ralph's eye is nearly swollen shut, and Eric's face is "a mask of dried blood" (p. 195). Piggy cannot see, and must be led by the arm. Ralph cannot get a fire going, making his decision the night before seem fateful. Ralph's abilities have diminished over the course of the past few chapters, and here he is so enraged and so confused by the loss of his authority that he requires Piggy to finish sentences for him. Piggy, for some reason, is emboldened by his blindness. He tells Ralph to call an assembly, even though it is absurd to do so. Sam rightly asks: "An assembly for only us?" (p. 196). When Ralph blows the conch, the narrator gives a short picture of the birds flying off: nature responding as it had the first day when he blew it. You might ask your students why Golding would include that short detail.

A couple of important details to notice about the speeches in this sad and pathetic assembly are Ralph's impotence and Piggy's boldness. They speak freely about what has been done, apparently freed from their own guilt by virtue of blaming Jack. Piggy holds fast to the rule of holding the conch to speak, a parliamentarian to the end. One particularly sad little detail is that, even in this situation, Piggy's nearest allies, Ralph and Samneric, laugh at him when he mentions his own inability to see. "Yes, laugh. Go on, laugh," he says (p. 197). It is Piggy who flatly states that Simon was murdered and who brings up the first death, the boy with the mulberry birthmark (p. 197). Piggy's assertion that he is going to tell off Jack Merridew brings the response, "You'll get hurt" (p. 197).

Piggy's response, "What can he do more than he has?" (p. 197) should also have brought a response from the others, and Piggy should remember what happened to Simon. Ask students to analyze Piggy's argument on page 198. Does Piggy have a point, or is he deluded? What is the significance of Piggy's crying as he makes his speech?

DISCUSSION/JOURNAL TOPIC: WHAT'S RIGHT'S RIGHT

In Piggy's speech at the top of page 198, he argues his intent to approach Jack and reason with him. Piggy's appeal, while counting on logic, also counts on a shared code of ethics, a notion of justice that is common to all the boys. Is his plan reasonable? What is wrong with it?

What are the signs that Piggy's idea to go see Jack is a bad one? Notice that the conch is again described as "fragile" (p. 198). When Ralph says to Piggy, "All right. I mean—you can try if you like. We'll go with you" (p. 198), he clearly does not think Piggy's argument is going to work. The conversation that follows shows the confusion of their situation. Samneric repeatedly warn that Jack's crew will be painted. Why does that matter? Ralph "dimly" remembers Simon telling him that he will get home all right, and perhaps takes confidence in that. He wants them to tidy up so that they look more civilized, perhaps wishing to appeal to the civilized memories of the others. But they have no means to tidy up. This section ends with a curious exchange between the boys, demonstrating Ralph's fading ability to think clearly. It is as though he has early onset dementia, and Piggy needs to remind him of rescue. Samneric appear to understand that there is a problem with Ralph, but they do not probe it further.

The next section of the chapter brings the boys to the Castle Rock for the confrontation, and this is another part of the book that you will want to read aloud in class, even if you have assigned it the night before. It moves quickly, and each line of the text includes some important detail that echoes events or descriptions that have already been given. The progression of the scene is as follows: the confrontation with Roger, Jack's return, Ralph's accusations, the first skirmish between Ralph and Jack, Ralph's plea for them to remember the signal fire, the abduction of the twins, the hand-to-hand fight between Ralph and Jack, Piggy's speech, the gathering of the tribe for a charge, Roger's release of the rock and Piggy's fall, and, finally, Jack's attack on Ralph.

Rather than walking through this section bit by bit, I want to point out a few details your students might look for, and that might provide insight into your reading. First, look for indications of Piggy's lack of safety. Think about why he is left crouching on a cliff with a 40-foot fall behind him when he cannot see. Notice that Piggy is terrified by where he is situated as much as by the confrontation. Notice under what conditions Piggy stands up, and what compels him to take the conch and make his stand. Second, look for indications of the growing savagery (or power) in the tribe, and in Roger particularly, as the scene progresses. How does the paint on their faces add to this growing power? For example, what does it mean when the narrator tells us that the painted boys felt the "otherness" of Samneric (p. 207)? Look for indications that they are still a group of boys, exhibiting the behavior of boys. Why do they cheer when Ralph and Jack fight? Also, look for descriptions that dehumanize Ralph, Piggy, and the twins. Why, for example, is Ralph "a shock of hair" and Piggy a "bag of fat" to Roger (p. 208)? How does this perception contribute to what happens? You will need also to address the description of Piggy's death, perhaps comparing it with the description of Simon's death.

Ironically, the death of Piggy may have saved Ralph. Notice this passage at the bottom of page 208:

> Now Jack was yelling too and Ralph could no longer make himself heard. Jack had backed right against the tribe and they were a solid mass of menace that bristled with spears. The intention of a charge was forming among them; they were working up to it and the neck would be swept clear. Ralph stood facing them, a little to one side, his spear ready.

If they had "swept the neck clear" then both Ralph and Piggy would have been doomed.

One other interesting detail at the end of the chapter involves Roger and Jack, who advance on Samneric. The final paragraph in the chapter shows Roger correcting Jack, apparently preparing to demonstrate a greater extent of cruelty than even Jack had manifested. Roger "edged past the chief, only just avoiding pushing him with his shoulder" (p. 211). This may indicate that Jack will not have to wait long before he faces a challenge to his authority. While the tribe appears to be a well-functioning authoritarian regime, they show here nothing but brutal impulsivity, which will lead them to destroy the island in the next chapter.

Twelve: Cry of the Hunters

The final chapter occupies itself, principally, with Ralph and his desperate attempt to avoid death at the hands of the savages. We no longer jump from one character to another, and despite any feelings or thoughts concerning Ralph's weaknesses or culpability in the deaths of Simon and Piggy, Golding puts the reader with Ralph exclusively until the jarring shift in narrative that introduces the naval officer and ends the book. The chapter divides into these sections:

1. Ralph wanders the island then returns to the Castle Rock
2. Interview between Ralph and Samneric
3. The hunt
4. The rescue

The chapter can be further subdivided, and it may be a good activity for your students to analyze the hunt section by dividing it into subparts. Like the chapter before it, however, this chapter moves very quickly, and even though it is laced with a large amount of description of the physical spaces, those descriptions are very familiar by this point, and thus do not impede the action. To the extent which we are able to cast ourselves into Ralph's situation, our hearts may race as does his own.

The first section begins with Ralph, immediately after escaping the savages following Piggy's death, examining his wounds. We see his filthiness and physical deterioration, which is ironic when we consider that he is the last civilized boy on the island, the rest having turned into savages. He looks up to the rock from which he has escaped. Notice how the other boys are described in this scene. The first is Bill, who you may recall was the last boy besides Samneric to defect to Jack's crew. Ralph cannot imagine that the savage he sees is actually Bill. Thus we see that, even in Ralph's mind, the boys are no longer themselves. The next boy he sees is Robert, who has also turned savage and stands guard, tossing a rock with one hand while holding his spear with the other. Remember that it was Robert who first showed Roger the mechanism of the lever and the rock that eventually killed Piggy.

In this segment, the boys are feasting again, which pains Ralph. He knows that Jack will not leave him alone, but he cannot believe they would actually hunt him, as he speaks out loud, "No. They're not as bad as that. It was an accident" (p. 213).

Ralph stumbles away from the scene, and we have an eerie segment that includes him scaring a couple of littluns and returning to the wrecked shelters on the beach. Thus we learn that absolutely no one is tending to the littluns—a point I will return to later. Ralph, almost Simon-like, decides that the only thing to do is return to the other boys and appeal to their sanity the next day.

On his way back to the Castle Rock, Ralph encounters what had been the Lord of the Flies, and as the feeling comes that the pig's head on a stick is something more than lifeless (recalling Simon's fit), Ralph tries to destroy it with his fists, only leaving the "grin" (p. 215) wider than he had found it. Ralph takes the spear—the first stick sharpened at both ends—and flees the scene.

Golding in this scene carefully describes the changes as the day shifts to night. Ralph thinks and thinks, and much of the narration in this chapter, particularly this section, concerns itself with Ralph's thoughts. At one point, he imagines that he can approach the others with a peace offering ("I've got pax," p. 215), but he soon realizes that won't work. As he works out this realization, he speaks out loud, "'Cos I had some sense" (p. 215), a quote that sounds quite similar to something Piggy would say, even in dialect.

DISCUSSION/JOURNAL TOPIC: RALPH'S THOUGHTS

Trace the development of Ralph as a thinker in *Lord of the Flies*. How does he think in the final chapter as opposed to earlier chapters? What causes his development as a thinker?

Ralph also senses his own stink, a stink made up of "salt and sweat and the staleness of dirt" (p. 215). As Ralph approaches the Castle Rock and sees again the death rock where Piggy had landed, he hears the chant of the savages and recognizes Samneric as the new guards of the castle. This realization comes as a turning point in his consideration of the situation. He realizes that there is no hope of forming his own society. He has lost all power. "There was no chance of rescuing them and building up an outlaw tribe at the other end of the island. Samneric were savages like the rest; Piggy was dead, and the conch smashed to powder" (p. 216). To his credit, Ralph refuses to believe his own thinking and thus chances discovery to approach and talk to Samneric. From here, the scene shifts to the second section.

DISCUSSION/JOURNAL TOPIC: THE CONCH

Have students discuss the conch. In the end, is the conch a symbol or not? What does it symbolize? What does its destruction symbolize? What keeps it from being symbolic, if anything?

In the beginning of the second section of Chapter 12, the table rock where Piggy had fallen is mentioned again, as the water of the ocean "breathed round the death rock and flowered into a field of whiteness" (p. 216). During Ralph's conversation with Samneric, the narrator returns to this description twice, heightening the sense of danger for Ralph and reminding us to hear, as readers, the continuous "breathing" of the waves (p. 216).

From the interview with Samneric, we learn the plot details that will drive the rest of the chapter. They will hunt Ralph at sunrise, spreading out in a line across the island, with a set of signals to follow. Roger is "a terror" (p. 220). Samneric have been subjected but have not lost their humanity (an important point). Most importantly, Roger has "sharpened a stick at both ends" (p. 220). Ralph is left to puzzle out the meaning of that phrase as he retreats. He pauses to consider, and feels his fatigue as though realizing it for the first time. Again the narrator mentions the table rock, but this time as a mocking mirage of bed and sheets. For a moment, the memory of Piggy makes Piggy the beast, "everywhere" become "terrible in darkness and death" (p. 221), and Ralph imagines him coming out of the water with his "empty head" (p. 221), an image that makes Ralph whimper like a littlun. Hearing voices above him, Ralph retreats to a hiding place nearby and hears Samneric being physically harmed. As he returns to his thoughts with the knowledge he has gained from them, he falls asleep.

The third section of this chapter is the climactic hunt. This scene represents the culmination of the development of Jack's tribe. As the chapter before marked the end of the civilized society that the boys tried to establish, as symbolized by the shattering of the conch, this scene marks the end of the hunting society, as they destroy the habitat necessary to sustain their hunting. Readers are shown the entire scene through the eyes of Ralph, and we experience the other characters only as sounds and occasional glimpses from various hiding places and chases. In one sense, Ralph, being hunted like a pig, shows us the perspective of the pigs on the island that have been hunted all along. Just as the very first pig gets hung up in the creepers, leading to Jack's first unsuccessful attempt to kill (see Chapter 1 of the novel), Ralph also gets hung up in creepers at one point, then breaks free in a panic, as did the pig.

Not only are the savages armed—Roger with a stick sharpened at both ends—but Ralph, too, has a stick sharpened at both ends, something that he has not yet realized. Have students trace the hunt in terms of its movements. First, the discovery of Ralph's first hiding place. Then, the heaving of the rocks, indicating that they are serious about killing him. If we have any sense that they are remorseful about what happened to Piggy, this segment would discount it, but again, we must remember that they are painted, which de-identifies them, and Ralph, in hiding, cannot be seen, so he could be crushed without their having to see him.

When the boys return to the spot where Ralph hides, having been unsuccessful at crushing him, Ralph makes his first attack, and although Golding does not identify the victim of Ralph's attack, I believe it is actually Jack he wounds, as Jack would be bold enough to stick his spear into the thicket, and the voice that says, "See? I told you—he's dangerous" (p. 225) is not Jack's. I assume that voice to belong to Roger, or perhaps Maurice. Another reason to believe the wounded savage is Jack is that the savages immediately set the fire to try to burn Ralph out of hiding, and it is Jack who has the means to start the fire. Golding is very careful in how he describes the starting of the fire. In an ecological reading, we would focus on all the descriptions of the fire in this chapter, and how it grows from this little trickle of smoke into the thundering apocalypse that devours the island.

Ralph escapes to the forest after attacking "like a cat," "snarling," as he stabs "a smallish savage" with his spear (p. 226). He leaves the savage doubled up, and we may wonder whether either of the two boys Ralph has attacked will make it out of the fire themselves. The next few pages move quickly, as Ralph runs from the fire and the line of hunters, thinking as he does so about his options. It is interesting that Golding's narrator grants Ralph the clarity to devise three options (climb a tree, break the line, or hide) and to pick his best option. Ralph, in survival mode, is at last learning to think.

Students reading this chase scene have many details to attend to: Ralph's thoughts, the description of the growing intensity of the fire, Ralph's relative position to the line of "ululations" (p. 226), and his actual movements. As Ralph finds his last hiding place, he achieves a kind of clarity. He understands the implications of the fire: "The fools! The fools! The fire must be almost at the fruit trees—what would they eat tomorrow?" (p. 230). But this thought is juxtaposed with the imminent danger: "A stick sharpened at both ends" (p. 230). We return to the growing fire, and Ralph witnesses the flight of the animals, indicating that perhaps that source of food will also perish in the fire.

As another savage approaches, Ralph discovers that his own spear is sharpened at both ends, which not only gives him a sort of primal courage, but also informs him of what fate is planned for him. In a stroke of brilliant writing, the narrator implies, through the repetition of "A stick sharpened" that the savage outside Ralph's hiding place is Roger, though he remains unnamed in the narrative. Ralph thinks of Simon's words to him—"You'll get back" (p. 231)—and he makes his last, mad charge at the savage. The pace of the narrative and the scene has reached its climax, as all the boys are running, along with the fire, bushes exploding, trees being eaten by flames, and Ralph becoming "fear" itself (p. 232).

DISCUSSION/JOURNAL TOPIC: FEAR REVISITED

We have seen how the fear in the boys—fear of darkness, fear of the beast, and fear of each other—has affected the events of the book. What is the significance of Ralph being described in the final chapter as "fear, hopeless fear on flying feet" (p. 232)? How does this image of Ralph becoming fear culminate the fear theme?

As Ralph reaches the beach and rolls over and over, expecting the end, begging for mercy, this section ends, and Golding brings in his deus ex machina.

The final section of the chapter and of the book shows an abrupt change in the narrative. Golding found this technique so successful that he employed it in his next two novels, *The Inheritors* and *Pincher Martin*. He forces us to immediately detach ourselves from the story as it has been told, right when we are in the midst of a heart-pounding, life-and-death hunt. These boys, described as bloodthirsty, menacing, snarling savages, are suddenly "a semicircle of little boys" (p. 233). But the naval officer does not take the situation seriously until he finds out that the boys have been killing each other. The strangeness of this scene makes it reflective of everything that has happened: the whole island burning down, the platform trees being consumed with flame, the officer remarking that the smoke from the fire had drawn their attention (so Jack's group was ironically successful at keeping a signal fire), Ralph needing "a bath, a haircut, a nose-wipe, and a good deal of ointment" (p. 233), other boys coming out of the forest, "with the distended bellies of small savages" (p. 233) and the symbolically pathetic attempt by Percival to recite his name and address.

Perhaps most extraordinary is the reduction of Jack, the heathen idol and chief, to "a little boy who wore the remains of an extraordinary black cap on his red hair and who carried the remains of a pair of spectacles at his waist" (p. 234). Ask your students how they interpret Jack's actions here: starting forward to claim his authority, then stopping after Ralph says that he is chief. Is Jack shamed out of his authority or is he smart to not step forward, especially given the officer's admonition of Ralph? The irony of the officer's statement that a group of British boys should have been able to "put up a better show than that" (p. 234) should remind your students of what Jack had said earlier about the English being "best at everything" (p. 44).

The book ends with the boys, perhaps all of them, weeping, following Ralph's lead, although it seems odd to believe that Jack and Roger would be capable of tears. This scene echoes a scene early in the book when all the littluns wept in terror, following Percival's lead. Ralph reaches the closest point he will come to enlightenment by grieving for the loss of Simon, the island, and most of all, Piggy.

The officer looks at his ship, reminding us that the boys will leave their little war and return to a world engaged in a grander version of it. As Golding said, "And who will rescue the adult and his cruiser?" (Epstein, 1997, p. 238).

Conclusion

This chapter has taken us through a first reading of the text, with discussion and journal ideas, activities, and commentary. Once your students have completed their first reading, they may want to have a summary discussion before moving on to formal writing or group project assignments. By all means, have that conversation, and if you are interested in innovative ways to facilitate study of the text following a first reading, the next chapter will present a number of ideas.

Chapter Materials

Name: _____ Date: _____

Student Activity Sheet #6:
The Wall of Notable Quotes

Applicable Portion of the Novel: All

Objectives:
1. Students will identify significant lines and quotes from *Lord of the Flies*.
2. Students will collaborate to build a reading of the novel.
3. Students will gather evidence to support their interpretations of the novel.

Common Core Standard(s): RL.9-10.1 and RL.9-10.4; RL.11-12.1 and RL.11-12.4

Directions: Keep a running log of quotes or specific lines from *Lord of the Flies* that you like. These should be short passages or phrases that you see as significant, interesting, or even confusing. We will post a large board on the wall of our classroom so that you may share favorite lines with your classmates, so that by the end of the first reading, the wall will be full of notable quotes. These lines could be quotes from characters or from the narrator. Below is a grid to help you.

Notable Quote	Character (or Narrator)	Page in Book

Student Activity Sheet #7:
Facts About Atomic Weapons

Applicable Portion of the Novel: Chapter 1

Objectives:
1. Students will investigate the Cold War and nuclear proliferation.
2. Students will connect the presence of nuclear weapons with their own sense of security.

Common Core Standard(s): RL.9-10.9, RH.9-10.1, and RS.9-10.1; RL.11-12.9, RH.11-12.1, and RS.11-12.1

Directions: Use our school's web resources to research World War II and the Cold War, and specifically seek information on atomic (i.e., nuclear) weapons. Bring at least two facts about the war and/or nuclear weapons to class to share.

Facts about WWII, the Cold War, and/or nuclear weapons:

_____

_____

_____

_____

_____

_____

_____

Reflection: How often, if at all, do you consider the presence of nuclear weapons in the world? What do you think of when you consider the presence of nuclear weapons?

_____

_____

_____

_____

_____

_____

_____

Student Activity Sheet #8:
Character Charts

Applicable Portion of the Novel: All

Objectives:

1. Students will identify character traits for the major characters in *Lord of the Flies*.
2. Students will analyze character motivations and character changes in the course of the novel.

Common Core Standard(s): RL.9-10.3, RL.11-12.3

Directions: Choose one of the formats presented on the following pages and take notes on the main characters throughout our reading of *Lord of the Flies*. Be ready to discuss your notes on characters in class with your peers.

Name: _____

Date: _____

Character Chart 1

Character	Positive Attributes	Negative Attributes	Motivated By	Fears	Overall Analysis
Ralph					
Jack					
Piggy					
Simon					
Roger					

Character Chart 2

Character	Key Quotes by Character	Key Actions by Character	What the Narrator Says About the Character	What Other Characters Say About the Character
Ralph				
Jack				
Piggy				
Simon				
Roger				

Name: _____ Date: _____

Student Activity Sheet #9:
Ecological Reading

Applicable Portion of the Novel: All

Objectives:
1. Students will understand the boys' agency in changing the ecology of the island.
2. Students will connect the boys' impact on their environment to their own effect on the environment through written reflection.

Common Core Standard(s): RL.9-10.1 and RL.9-10.2; RL.11-12.1 and RL.11-12.2

Directions: As you work through *Lord of the Flies*, list descriptions and actions that indicate the effect the boys have on the ecology of the island, from their use of the island's resources to their difficulties in surviving there. Having the list will aid you in writing in response to the text and project work. The word "agency" refers to the object, tool, or means by which the characters make their environmental impact. An example has been provided.

Effect on the Island	Character(s) and Agency	Chapter and Page Number
Scar smashed into the island	Pilot, airplane	Chapter 1, page 1

Student Activity Sheet #10:
Staging Conflict

Applicable Portion of the Novel: Chapter 3, pages 53–54

Objectives:
1. Students will demonstrate understanding of an excerpt of the novel through theatrical staging.
2. Students will engage in kinesthetic learning by connecting movement with comprehension.

Common Core Standard(s): RL.9-10.7, SL.9-10.6; RL.11-12.7

Directions:
Working in groups of three, take the dialogue from Jack and Ralph on pages 53–54, write it out as speeches in a script, and then take the narration and format it as stage directions. The conversation vacillates between friendly, casual talk and angry, resentful arguing. Once you have translated the dialogue into script format, rehearse the scene as a group. Groups will be chosen to perform the scene in class.

Notes:

_____

_____

_____

_____

_____

_____

_____

_____

_____

_____

_____

_____

_____

_____

_____

_____

_____

_____

Student Activity Sheet #11:
Collage of Tropical Vegetation

Applicable Portion of the Novel: All

Objectives:
1. Students will gather and organize visual representations of the setting in *Lord of the Flies*.
2. Students will collaborate to produce a collage of images that communicates their impression of the island.

Common Core Standard(s): RL.9-10.7 and RL.9-10.1; RL 11-12.7 and RL 11-12.1

Directions: Find at least two pictures of jungle or tropical island scenery and bring them to class. We will create a class collage of images and post it near the Wall of Notable Quotes. In the space below, give your photos titles and comment on how they represent the story. You may also connect each photo to one of the quotes on the Wall of Notable Quotes, or find other quotes in the novel that represent your photos.

Photo/Image 1

Title:_____

Connection to Novel:

_____

_____

_____

_____

_____

Photo/Image 2

Title:_____

Connection to Novel:

_____

_____

_____

_____

_____

Name: _____ Date: _____

Student Activity Sheet #12:
Jigsaw for Chapter 4

Applicable Portion of the Novel: Chapter 4

Objectives:
1. Students will analyze portions of one chapter as a group.
2. Students will share interpretations with peers.
3. Students will construct a whole picture of a chapter of difficult text based on the several sections they have studied
4. Students will demonstrate individual authority over sections of the text through expert reading and sharing.

Common Core Standard(s): RL.9-10.1, RL.9-10.5, and SL.9-10.1; RL.11-12.1, RL 11-12.5, and SL.11-12.1

Directions: For this activity, we will divide into 8 different groups, each assigned one of the eight divisions in Chapter 4 of *Lord of the Flies*. Each group will discuss their chosen section of the chapter and generate interpretive statements of what the section is about. Look for main ideas and details to support them. We will then regroup into 3 larger groups, each one having a representative of each of the 8 smaller groups. Students in these second groups will take turns sharing the interpretive statements from the smaller groups and discussing thoughts on the chapter as a whole. Each group will generate a list of important ideas from the chapter.

The eight divisions of Chapter 4 are:
1. A summary of the boys' situation
2. A focus on three littluns, Roger, and Maurice
3. Henry on the beach and Roger throwing the rocks
4. Jack paints his face
5. Ralph and Piggy: an uneasy relationship
6. Ralph sees the ship and runs to the mountain
7. Confrontation between Ralph, Jack, and Piggy on the mountain
8. The boys roast and eat a pig

Student Activity Sheet #13:
Blocking the Confrontation on the Mountain

Applicable Portion of the Novel: Chapter 4

Objectives:
1. Students will picture the movement of characters in a specific scene of the novel.
2. Students will connect physical movement with emotional content in the scene.
3. Students will articulate their comprehension of the reading through movement, discussion, and writing.

Common Core Standard(s): RL.9-10.7, RL.11-12.1

Directions: Following the spotting of the ship and the discovery that the signal fire has gone out, Ralph, Piggy, Bill, and Simon run up the mountain to find that the signal fire has gone out. When Jack and his hunters return from their hunt, the boys have a tense conversation that leads to Jack hitting Piggy and breaking his glasses (pp. 74–82).

Working in pairs or a small group, take this scene and "block" out movement for each of the characters. You can do this in writing or by drawing pictures that indicate movement and when in the scene the movement occurs.

Example:

Page 77, line 10:
Jack is kneeling over the dead pig, and he has his back to Piggy and Ralph. He says, "The job was too much. We needed everyone." He looks around at everyone and goes back to looking at the pig, ignoring Ralph.

_____

_____

_____

_____

_____

_____

_____

_____

_____

_____

Student Activity Sheet #14:
Appreciating Golding: A Lesson in Descriptive Writing

Applicable Portion of the Novel: Chapter 5

Objectives:
1. Students will understand author's craft of pacing and description.
2. Students will demonstrate ability to detail a scene and the relationship between scene and character.

Common Core Standard(s): RL.9-10.5 and W.9-10.3; RL.11-12.5, W.11-12.3b, and W.11-12.3d

Directions: On pages 84–86 of *Lord of the Flies*, the narrator describes the assembly platform as it appears to Ralph in the evening. Count the number of sentences that describe the platform or some individual detail found there, how many sentences describe the thoughts of Ralph, and how many sentences tell of an action occurring. After class discussion of these sentences, narrate a story with three to five actions. The actions can be as small as someone moving an arm or taking a step. Between each action in the story, you must include three to five sentences of description.

_____

_____

_____

_____

_____

_____

_____

_____

_____

_____

_____

_____

Reflection: What have you learned about descriptive writing from doing this exercise?

_____

_____

_____

_____

Student Activity Sheet #15:
Who Believes in the Beast?

Applicable Portion of the Novel: Chapter 5

Objectives:
1. Students will analyze character differences using the theme of fear in *Lord of the Flies*.
2. Students will write character notes to help track developments in their understanding of the "fear" theme in the novel.

Common Core Standard(s): RL.9-10.2 and RL.9-10.3; RL.11-12.3

Directions: Use the chart below to indicate different characters' attitudes toward "the beast." Write notes on what each character thinks about the beast, and use the final column to indicate any changes in the characters' attitude or beliefs that take place as the story progresses.

Character	Thoughts on the Beast	Changes?
Ralph		
Jack		
Piggy		
Simon		
Roger		
Maurice		
Other		

Student Activity Sheet #16:
Plato's "Allegory of the Cave"

Applicable Portion of the Novel: Chapters 8–9

Objectives:
1. Students will read and comprehend a challenging classical text.
2. Students will connect Plato's "Allegory of the Cave" to the story of Simon in *Lord of the Flies*.
3. Students will consider the role of learned people and spiritual leaders in society.

Common Core Standard(s): RL.9-10.3, RL.9-10.9, RI.9-10.1, and W.9-10.9; RL.11-12.2, RL.11-12.7, W.11-12.2

Directions: Another way to look at Simon is as the hypothetical figure in Plato's "Allegory of the Cave" who is released from bondage and permitted to see the truth. Access any print or online version of the allegory. Read Plato's allegory and construct parallels between the figure in the allegory who is permitted to leave the cave and Simon in *Lord of the Flies*. Use the two-column grid below or a similar two-column page in your journal. We will discuss the parallels in class.

Plato's "Allegory of the Cave"	Simon in *Lord of the Flies*
Description:	Description:
Similarities:	

Name: _____   Date: _____

Student Activity Sheet #17:
Movie Madness

Applicable Portion of the Novel: Simon's death, Chapter 9

Objectives:
1. Students will examine two film interpretations of a specific scene in *Lord of the Flies*.
2. Students will analyze the directorial choices and how those choices influence the emotional impact of the scene.

Common Core Standard(s): RL.9-10.7; RL.11-12.7

Directions: In class we will view the movie version of Simon's death from the 1963 film *Lord of the Flies*, directed by Peter Brook. Below, write what effects the elements of the scene have on you. Consider the soundtrack, the images, the dialogue, and the movement. We will then watch the same scene from the 1990 film version (dir. Harry Hook), and you will repeat the exercise. As a class, we will discuss these cinematic representations of the scene.

Film clip 1 (1963)
Notes:

_____

_____

_____

_____

_____

_____

_____

Film clip 2 (1990)
Notes:

_____

_____

_____

_____

_____

_____

_____

"This is what people can talk about": Discussing and Performing *Lord of the Flies*

The best classrooms are those that are driven by student questions, not teacher questions (Eisner, 2001). While I present a large volume of prompts and questions throughout this text, I also encourage you to develop in your students the ability to drive discussions through their own questions raised by their reading and interaction with *Lord of the Flies*. If you can get your students to the place where they are asking questions of each other and you, questions that lead everyone back to the text and out into the culture that is reflected in the text, then you will be successful regardless of whichever ideas you choose to use from this book.

Lord of the Flies is an excellent novel to discuss with students, and one of the reasons why it was so popular on college campuses in the 1960s (*Time*, 1962) and remains so today is that it invites many different readings, from the philosophical to the social, theological, and symbolic. Beyond the several discussion ideas presented in Chapter 4 to support a first reading of the text, this chapter presents ideas for postreading discussion and in-class performance both to extend students' understanding and to prepare them for writing and project work in connection with the novel. Indeed, many of the discussions presented in this chapter may serve as writing exercises or paper topics. I first present discussion ideas based on traditional literary elements, followed by debate topics and performance ideas that spark discussion and writing. Finally, I include a list of additional discussion/ journaling questions and topics for each chapter.

Comprehension Discussions
Using Literary Elements

Discussions of Setting

Golding's island may be considered a character in its own right, the descriptions are so detailed and the boys' struggles with the island so numerous. How is the island nurturing to the boys, and how is it threatening? What specific features cause them hardship, and what features facilitate their pleasure? Differentiate between the three main locales on the island: the beach/platform, the mountain, and the Castle Rock. What happens at these different places? How does the geographical isolation of the island influence the boys? What qualities are attributed to the ocean throughout the book, from the power of the waves crashing on the rocks to the phosphorescent caressing of Simon's body? Have students explore these and other aspects of setting. Bring in pictures (such as in the collage activity in Chapter 4, SAS #11) of tropical islands or vegetation to help students visualize the island.

Discussions of Conflict

The best way to approach conflict in discussion is to have students generate a list of conflicts they perceive in the novel, share them with each other in small groups, and then collate the list for whole-group discussion. Every conflict will have development points, turning points, and outcomes, so an early conversation of conflicts, many of which are established by the end of Chapter 2 in the story, can provide material for later discussions. Students can generate visual representations of conflict and post them on the classroom wall. As new conflicts emerge in the novel, students can add those conflicts to the list.

ACTIVITY (SAS #18): CONFLICT

Have students choose a conflict in *Lord of the Flies* that interests them. Have them generate a visual representation of the conflict, tracing events in the novel that develop the conflict. Their visual representations may take the form of a timeline, a circle, a map, or any other form that best illustrates the conflict. For example, students can trace the conflict between Ralph and Jack by marking pivotal events in their encounters as spots on a game board. As a class, gather the list of conflicts students have generated. Have students discuss the conflict list and determine which conflicts have the most importance in the story.

Using a computer, tablet, or iPad, you can record the lists generated and make notes on the discussion of conflict, then return to the list for reference in later discussions or projects. Identifying conflicts can give students a sense of purpose when reading and rereading various scenes. Here are a few of the more predominant conflicts your students may identify: Ralph versus Jack, work versus play (or responsibility versus freedom), signal fire versus hunting, democracy versus dictatorship, order versus chaos, Jack versus Piggy, Simon versus his emotions, the boys versus fear of the beast, and the boys versus the island.

Discussions of Character

Students are naturally drawn to characters, and they will form impressions of characters before they analyze plot or theme. They will look for recognition of personality traits exhibited by the characters as compared to the people they know or other characters they have read about. What the character says, what the character does, how the character is described by the narrator, and how the character is described by other characters all contribute to our understanding. Finally, our reading of secondary sources will illuminate our interpretations (see Chapter 6). As students examine character in class discussion, you might set up the character analysis as a series of dichotomies or opposites. For example, you might look for good leadership qualities in Ralph versus poor leadership qualities, positive aspects of Jack's personality versus negative aspects, ways that Piggy is annoying versus ways that he makes positive contributions, signs of strength in Simon versus signs of weakness, and so on. If students struggle with interpretation of characters, the avenues I have mentioned here may be rendered as a grid for visualization, using the character charts (see SAS #8 in Chapter 4).

Discussions of Narrative Point of View

The narrator plays a large role in this book, and is not limited in the omniscience he reveals (I say "he" simply because the author is male, understanding that in *Lord of the Flies*, the narrator is an extension of the author, although not necessarily the author himself). The narrator takes us variously into the minds of the different characters and occasionally into the collective mindset of the boys. Students can and should discuss narrative structure in the book and point of view. In particular (as discussed in Chapter 4), students may notice the narrative shifts between simultaneous scenes on the island. One moment we are with Jack, then with Ralph and Piggy, and perhaps then with Simon. Have students discuss what these narrative shifts accomplish. Also, have students isolate instances where the narrator steps in to affect our perception of a character or a situation by evaluating rather than simply describing. For example, consider this passage describing

Ralph: "You could see now that he might make a boxer, as far as width and heaviness of shoulders went, but there was a mildness about his mouth and eyes that proclaimed no devil" (p. 5). Compare that with this description of Jack: "His face was crumpled and freckled, and ugly without silliness. Out of this face stared two light blue eyes, frustrated now, and turning, or ready to turn, to anger" (p. 17).

As students work through the novel, they may want to think of the narrator as a documentary filmmaker, who holds the camera while telling us what he observes. This documentarian has the added talent of getting inside the heads of his subjects, but he is selective about how he does it. He does not, for example spend much time inside Roger's head, only hinting at subtle changes in his consciousness, such as when he throws the rocks around Henry or when he understands the beating of Wilfred as "an illumination" that causes him to assimilate "the possibilities of irresponsible authority" (p. 184).

Discussions of Plot

Students may want to talk simply about what happens in the story, the actions of the characters, and the way that actions build conflict and move the story forward. The narrative is difficult enough that there may be disagreement over actual events in the story, or over who says what, especially when an individual speaker is not identified, as often is the case during assemblies. In particular, when reviewing certain scenes, such as the scene when Ralph, Jack, and Roger approach the beast on the mountain, you will want to establish order of events specifically with your students.

It often helps to build a plotline as a large visual on the classroom wall, so the students can refer to it as they progress through the unit. During the initial read-through, have students agree upon and then mark on the plotline the actions and the dialogue that are important. When they have finished their first reading and are working on projects and essays, the visual reminder of the important events in the plot will be helpful to them.

ACTIVITY (SAS #19): PLOTLINE

A good way to keep students on track with plot is to assign them to develop a plotline, like a timeline of the story, with all events we know of added as they occur in the reading. You can make a big plotline and post it on the wall of your classroom, having students add to it as they progress through their unit on *Lord of the Flies*. Or you can have students construct their own plotlines and include the events they see as most important. Good discussion can grow from having students summarize action and rank plot events in terms of their importance to the different characters or conflicts. They can also match the plotline with their conflict illustrations described above or with excerpts from the Wall of Notable Quotes. These notations will be good tools for later written analyses.

Of course, plot is not simply the order of events in the story. It is the connection of events in a purposeful progression that builds theme, so it will be good to ask students to summarize the events into an identification of "What is the plot?" which points us in the direction of the follow-up question: "What is the theme?"

Discussions of Theme

Lord of the Flies offers a number of tantalizing themes to discuss, and ultimately when students are asked to write interpretive essays, they often must connect whatever literary elements they choose to address to the book's overall meaning or significance, which, of course, necessitates a grasp of theme. Identifying themes in the text allows us to go backwards into events, descriptions, symbols, and other textual elements, then to go forward into interpretation of what the text has to say about the themes it presents.

School readings are by their nature situated, as the student reader does not encounter the text in a void, nor does he or she encounter the text alone, which ultimately alters the student's experience with the text. Teachers often have discussion agendas and interpretive agendas that they coerce their students into accepting, even if those agendas stand at odds with what the student's organic, unmediated reading might be. Classroom discussion serves as a mediating force in student readings, but teachers can avoid the pitfall of exerting interpretive and discursive dominance (Neal, 2008) by opening discussion to themes that resonate with students, and allowing students the time to develop those discussions.

Below are some themes that may work well in discussion and essay composition, together with descriptions and discussion questions related to them. There will inevitably be overlap between these themes and discussions.

- *Fear*—How does fear first present itself? What is the nature of the boys' fear, and how realistic is that fear? How does the littluns' fear affect the biguns? What is the difference between Jack's fear and Piggy's fear? Are any of the boys immune from fear, and if so, how?

- *Power*—Who has nominal power on the island? Who has symbolic power? Who has actual power? How is power distributed and understood by the boys? How does the balance of power shift during the story? How are the power relationships in the story emblematic of adult society?

- *Good and evil*—What is the nature of good and evil in the story? How is goodness represented? How is evil represented? What events in the story are the results of good intent? What events reveal bad intent? What does *Lord of the Flies* ultimately say to us about good and evil? How valid is the book's presentation of good and evil? Do the concepts of good and evil have validity in themselves?

- *Survival*—What does survival mean in the story? What does it mean to the different characters? What threatens the boys' survival? What aids in their survival?

- *Political organization*—The semidemocratic society represented by the whole group early in the book can be contrasted with the authoritarian society of Jack's tribe later in the book. How should the boys organize themselves?

- *Human nature*—The novel asks fundamental questions about human nature. Who are we? Are we naturally good or naturally bad? How does the book answer these questions, and what do we think about those answers?

- *War and peace*—The boys descend into savagery and war by the book's end, but they are in some ways only mimicking a larger war being fought among nations. What are the forces of war and peace in the novel, and are they realistic? What is necessary for peace to exist among the boys?

- *Light and darkness*—Track the references to day and night, and light and darkness, as they appear in the narration. How are the representations of different times of the day echoed in the characters themselves?

- *Civil rights*—Who has rights on the island? How are those rights exercised, and how are they taken away? Who has the right to speak and who has the right to act?

- *Bullying*—What is the connection between Piggy's mistreatment and the book's outcome? How is Piggy an archetype of children who face bullying and intimidation every day?

- *Religion*—How does Golding's tale reveal a theological stance? Is this a Christian tale? A broadly spiritual tale? What in nature is spiritual and what is existentially indifferent?

- *Cooperation and conflict*—How do the boys understand cooperation and its importance? What is the value of conflict between boys on the island?

- *Ecology*—What does the conflict between the boys and the island tell us about human impact on the environment?

- *Grief*—How does Golding's claim that the theme of the book is "grief" (Golding, 1982, p. 163) work for your students? Was Golding right about his own book?

Think about which of these themes you would like to explore with your students, as well as others that may be potentially missing from this list.

Discussions of Symbols

Few novels present symbolic objects and characters as clearly as does *Lord of the Flies*. The novel has been called an allegory (Dickson, 1990), though Golding himself preferred the term "fable" or better yet, "myth," due to the representational nature of the characters and the realia presented on the island. While the book may not have yet achieved mythic status, the characters have become, in my view, archetypes of modern personalities and roles, not only in youth society, but also in society as a whole. On the other hand, the realism with which the characters are drawn and the events are told in some way prevents us from being able to neatly categorize them symbolically and reduce them to representations, such as Simon as a symbol of love, Christ, or goodness; Jack as a symbol of hate, power, or the devil; Roger as violence, chaos, or evil; Ralph as politics or human inadequacy; or Piggy as a symbol of reason and intelligence. As Sugimura (2008) contended, the symbols at some point cease to be symbolic because Golding forces us to see the boys fully, particularly at the book's end. But *Lord of the Flies* contains both human and nonhuman symbols that allow teachers to examine with students the nature of symbolism and to make operational for the students the term "symbol" in literature.

Below is a list of characters, objects, and actions from the text that may be interpreted as symbols. I will leave it to you and your students to explore how these characters, objects, and actions are symbolic, and how they may ultimately escape symbolization. You may discuss these using a whole-class approach, tossing out the item or name and asking students to generate ideas for what they symbolize. Another, perhaps better, approach might be to split students into groups and give each group one or two potential symbols to examine. A still better approach, and the most student centered, would be to pick one symbol, such as the conch, discuss it with your students, then have them generate their own list of potential symbols from the text, explaining their choices to the larger group. You might say of the conch that it becomes a symbol of civility or order; that it symbolizes the transformation of the natural into the useful; and that, in its destruction, it becomes symbolic of the failure of society in the face of natural brutality. Here are other possible symbols that your students may be given or that they may generate themselves:

- *Physical features*—the island, the scar, the conch, the platform, the unbalanced log, the mountain, the lagoon, the creepers, the heat, the storm, the balancing rocks, the ocean, the bower, the fruit, the pigs, the meat

- *Found and used objects*—the conch, the face paint, the pig's head (Lord of the Flies), the shelters, the stick sharpened at both ends, the dead parachutist

- ❦ *Human features*—Piggy's glasses, clothing, long hair, dirty bodies, Ralph's fingernails, diarrhea, Jack's cap, Piggy's fat, Jack's ugliness, Ralph's good looks, Roger's dark features, Simon's bright eyes, Simon's fainting, Percival's lack of memory, Ralph's tears

- ❦ *Characters*—Ralph, Jack, Piggy, Simon, Roger, Samneric, Percival, the boy with the mulberry-colored birthmark, the dead parachutist, the naval officer

- ❦ *Events or actions*—The calling of assembly, voting for chief, division of labor, the making of fire, Simon feeding the littluns, the inability to keep fire going, hunting, the killing of the sow, leaving the pig's head on a stick, the killing of Simon, the killing of Piggy, the shattering of the conch, the burning of the island

- ❦ *Other*—the beast, the battleship

While certainly an argument may be made for any of the things listed above as symbolic, we may also argue against their status as symbols, and that is what makes symbol a fruitful topic for class discussion and writing. In arguing whether an object or entity in the book works on a symbolic level, students are forced back into the text to trace the different appearances or mentions of that object or entity, engaging in the kind of interpretive discourse that develops analytical thinking and prepares them for writing well-supported argumentative essays. After all, once we agree that a feature in the book is symbolic and identify what that symbol signifies, then we can address the validity of that signification against our existing worldview, leading us to consider, accept, or reject what Golding presents to us.

If students want to present artistic visual representations of the symbols, have them do so along with text explanations and quotes from the text.

Debates

Engaging students in debate around situations and issues presented in the text is a way to get them thinking critically about the story and engaging in intellectual activity that is critical to the Common Core: specifically, citing textual evidence to support interpretation and pursuing secondary informational text. The following debate topics may be addressed informally in class discussion or with more extensive preparation and formal treatment. My goal is that you will incorporate topics that make sense to you into your unit design and then provide the tools for your students to build their arguments for debate. For example, you may encourage students to prepare for the debates by consulting critical essays on the book (see Chapter 8 for a list of such works). The connection between these debate topics and further argumentative writing assignments is obvious, but that will also depend upon your learning objectives.

You will need to choose whether these debates will take place as whole-class or small-group activities, and also whether students should choose sides based on their convictions or will have their positions randomly assigned. Also, you will determine when in the progression of the unit is the best time to hold these debates. Some topics below may be addressed during the first reading of the text and some may be best held following a complete first reading.

Debate Topic 1: Who Is the Better Leader, Ralph or Jack?

Have students look into the text to find specific situations where both boys show good leadership skills or poor leadership skills based upon the students' own notions of what qualities a good leader should have. You may refer them back to the prereading activity in Chapter 3 of this book, wherein they developed a list of qualities a good leader should have. In preparing for the debate, students may also read secondary materials on leadership.

Debate Topic 2: What is More Important, Keeping a Signal Fire or Finding Meat?

This topic is related to Topic 1 in that the side students take will perhaps relate to their position on who is the better leader between Ralph and Jack. Students should prepare by examining Maslow's hierarchy of needs (see Chapter 3 of this book) and by examining the comfort level of the boys in relation to their physical needs. Things for them to consider are the likelihood of rescue versus the insistence of hunger, the chronic diarrhea that the boys have from eating fruit, and the benefits of cooperation in a society.

Debate Topic 3: Is Ralph's Outrage Justified or Not?

Ralph becomes enraged when a ship passes by and the signal fire is not visible, as Jack and his hunters were achieving their first kill (Chapter 4 of the novel). One of Ralph's possible leadership errors is his unwillingness to forgive Jack and the hunters for letting the fire go out. Even Samneric think Ralph is "waxy" about the fire (Chapter 6, p. 108). But is Ralph right to be outraged by their behavior?

Debate Topic 4: Is Jack's Rebellion Justified or Not?

Jack provides meat that all the boys eat, including Ralph and Piggy. He apologizes for letting the fire go out, and he is brave enough to hunt for the beast. Is Jack right for splitting off from Ralph's group and forming his own group (Chapter 8), or should he stay and work things out with Ralph and the others? Does his behavior toward Piggy influence our thinking?

Debate Topic 5: Does Piggy Have a Legitimate Role in Governing the Group?

Piggy refuses to work, he badgers the others, and he does not enjoy the respect of anyone except possibly Ralph and Simon. He fails at his one responsibility, which is to number and keep track of the littluns. But he also demonstrates intelligence, encourages the boys to act like grownups, and supports Ralph. Does Piggy have a legitimate role in the governance of the group, or should he not have any say in the government on the island?

Debate Topic 6: Is Humanity Naturally Good or Naturally Evil?

This is a return to one of the prereading topics mentioned in Chapter 3 of this book, but using the novel as a core text to frame the debate. You could frame this as a Rousseau versus Hobbes debate, but I would caution you to have students gather information on these two philosophers rather than simply framing the argument as "Rousseau believed man is naturally good and Hobbes believed man is naturally evil." What may be more relevant to a discussion of the boys' society is Rousseau's notion of the necessity of community to successful political organization, as opposed to Hobbes's notion of the necessity of a sovereign authority to prevent war, which he saw as a natural state, from occurring. Encourage students to investigate the two viewpoints, but frame it in simple terms, such as: "What is more important to the boys' survival: that they work together as a community or that they obey the authority of their chosen leader?" Students may naturally believe that working as a community is always better, but the opposite side may point out that Jack's tribe works well as a community, although it does terrible things. Likewise, following the rule of the leader is preferable in their situation if the leader is issuing reasonable edicts.

Debate Topic 7: Are All of the Boys Responsible for Simon's Death, or Only a Few?

Either following the reading of Chapters 9 and 10 or after the first complete read-through of the story, debate whether Jack and the tribe are guilty of murder or whether Simon caused his own death through misjudgment. Have both sides take a position on whether Ralph and Piggy are guilty as well.

Reader's Theatre

The Reader's Theatre activity works well as a way to bring performance into your classroom study of *Lord of the Flies*. Typically, a group of students presents a scene from the book that they have converted to dialogue, with narration optional. Some narration may be necessary, but narration that describes tone of voice or emotion may be cut and instead included as stage directions for the performers. Student performers stand at the front of the room and read the scene as though they are actors who will bring emotion to the speeches, but not movement. It is common and, if possible, desirable to give the students microphones to use during the reading, but the activity can be successful without them, too. A good rule of thumb is to do a 5–10 minute reading, and then have the class discuss what they hear in the reading. You may even do a Reader's Theatre activity as a prereading exercise, and the sample script that follows may be used in that way.

Essentially any one of the assembly scenes makes a good candidate for Reader's Theatre, as well as smaller scenes that are rich with dialogue, such as the scene between Jack and Ralph (with Simon) early in Chapter 3. Pages 130–132 include a Reader's Theatre script for the second assembly, from the beginning of Chapter 2, as a sample. As you work through the novel yourself, identify other scenes that you can imagine would work well for your students. Students can create a small Reader's Theatre script as an auxiliary assignment or as an end of unit project, depending upon your unit structure.

Tableau Revisited

This simple activity asks students to create a picture of a stage scene from a certain moment in the script using themselves as the characters. Students can choose their own moments to portray and can add everything from costumes to background and props. They need only present the tableau to their peers and allow their peers to study it and talk about it. Students should be able to defend their choices. You can stop classroom reading or discussion of a scene at any time and construct the picture with the students as a sort of laboratory activity. A simple "What does this look like on stage?" can initiate a 5–10 minute tableau vivant activity that allows students to argue for what they see in their mind's eye as they work through the script.

Reader's Theatre: Sample

Assembly at Beginning of Chapter 2
Characters: Ralph, Jack, Simon, Piggy, Chorus (2–3 boys), Little Boy (with mulberry-colored birthmark), Narrator

Narrator:	Scene, the assembly platform on a tropical island. Ralph, the newly elected leader, has the conch. He, Jack, and Simon have just returned from their first exploration of the island. The boys are making noise, and Ralph must get their attention.
Chorus:	(*murmuring*)
Ralph:	(*clears throat*) Ahem! Well then.
Chorus:	(*all become quiet*)
Ralph:	Well then. We're on an island. We've been on the mountain top and seen water all round. We saw no houses, no smoke, no footprints, no boats, no people. We're on an uninhabited island with no other people on it.
Jack:	(*interrupting*) All the same you need an army—for hunting. Hunting pigs—
Ralph:	Yes, there are pigs on the island.
Jack:	We saw—
Simon:	Squealing—
Ralph:	It broke away—
Jack:	Before I could kill it—but—next time!
Narrator:	Jack slams his knife into a trunk and looks around challengingly.
Chorus:	(*makes some noise, then settles down*)
Ralph:	So you see, we need hunters to get us meat. And another thing. (*looking around at the boys*) There aren't any grownups. We shall have to look after ourselves.
Chorus:	(*makes some noise, then settles down*)
Ralph:	And another thing. We can't have everybody talking at once. We'll have to have "hands up" like at school.
Narrator:	Ralph holds up the conch.
Ralph:	Then I'll give him the conch.
Simon:	Conch?
Ralph:	That's what this shell's called. I'll give the conch to the next person to speak. He can hold it when he's speaking.
Chorus:	But—Look—
Ralph:	And he won't be interrupted. Except by me.
Narrator:	Jack jumps to his feet.

Jack:	We'll have rules! Lots of rules! Then when anyone breaks 'em—
Chorus:	(*viciously, as though hitting someone*) Whee—oh!
Jack:	Wacco!
Chorus:	Bong!
Jack:	Doink!
Narrator:	Piggy takes the conch from Ralph's lap.
Piggy:	(*shouting*) You're hindering Ralph. You're not letting him get to the most important thing. (*pauses*) Who knows we're here, eh?
Jack:	(*derisively*) They knew at the airport.
Chorus:	The man with the trumpet thing.
Ralph:	My dad.
Piggy:	(*shouting in high voice*) Nobody knows we're here. (*out of breath*) Perhaps they know where we was going to, and perhaps not. But they don't know where we are 'cos we never got there.
Narrator:	Piggy sits down.
Ralph:	That's what I was going to say, when you all, all . . . (*looking around*) The plane was shot down in flames. Nobody knows where we are. We may be here a long time. (*pauses*) A long time. (*pauses, then changes to a happy tone*) But this is a good island. There's food and drink and—
Jack:	Rocks!
Simon:	Blue flowers!
Ralph:	This is our island. Until the grownups come to fetch us we'll have fun.
Narrator:	Jack takes the conch.
Jack:	There's pigs. There's food, and bathing water in that little stream there—and everything. Didn't anyone find anything else?
Narrator:	Suddenly, a little boy with a mulberry-colored birthmark on his face comes forward.
Little Boy:	(*barely audible*) The snake thing.
Chorus:	Speak up.
Little Boy:	(*barely audible*) The snake thing.
Chorus:	(*laughing*) Speak up.
Piggy:	(*shouting*) Let him have the conch! Let him have it!
Narrator:	The little boy stands silently, so Piggy kneels down and lets the boy whisper in his ear.
Piggy:	He wants to know what you're going to do about the snake-thing.
All:	(*break into laughter*)

Ralph:	Tell us about the snake-thing.
Piggy:	Now he says it was a beastie.
Jack:	Beastie?
Piggy:	A snake-thing. Ever so big. He saw it.
Ralph:	Where?
Piggy:	In the woods.
Ralph:	You couldn't have a beastie, a snake-thing on an island this size.
Piggy:	He says it came in the dark.
Chorus:	(*murmurs*)
Ralph:	Then he couldn't see it!
Piggy:	He still says he saw the beastie. It came and went away again and came back and wanted to eat him—
Simon:	He was dreaming.
Ralph:	He must have had a nightmare. Stumbling about among those creepers—
Chorus:	(*murmurs*)
Piggy:	He says will it come back tonight?
Ralph:	(*voice rising*) But there isn't a beastie!
Jack:	Ralph's right of course. There isn't a snake-thing. But if there was a snake we'd hunt it and kill it. We're going to hunt pigs and get meat for everybody. And we'll look for the snake, too—
Ralph:	(*shouting*) But there isn't a snake!
Jack:	We'll make sure when we go hunting.
Chorus:	(*cheers*)
Ralph:	But there isn't a snake!

END SCENE

Theatrical Representations and Multimedia Performance

Following from the Reader's Theatre activity, students who are so inclined can develop actual performances of scenes from the novel, and if given time, can incorporate elements of media, such as film, music, and set. YouTube is already teeming with student drama related to *Lord of the Flies*, and while you and your students may amuse yourselves by examining some of these already-available samples, constructing your own depictions of the scenes will be more rewarding. As a follow-up to such theatrical and media-based creative work, students may write about how their skit or film is based on a certain interpretation of the novel. Thus, the visual work is grounded in analysis.

Additional Multilevel Discussion/Writing Topics

The categories of these discussion topics are modeled on Raphael's (1986) Question/Answer Relationships (QAR), with important changes. In lieu of the categories of increasing intellectual demand inherent in typical QAR strategies ("right there," "think and search," "author and me," "on my own"), I choose to use the categories of "comprehend," "connect," "extend," and "imagine" to cover increasing levels of thinking from Bloom's taxonomy, and also to combine interpretation with creative thinking.

Chapter 1

Comprehend
1. Summarize the description of the island in the opening scene.
2. What is Ralph's attitude toward Piggy?
3. How is Jack described?
4. How do the boys react to Simon's fainting spell?
5. Why is Piggy upset with Ralph before Ralph leaves with Jack and Simon?
6. What prevents Jack from killing the piglet?

Connect
1. What is the difference between Ralph's assessment of the situation and Piggy's?
2. Explain the imagery the narrator uses to describe the choir.
3. Compare Ralph with Jack.

Extend

1. Describe a situation you have been in where you felt out of place and compare it with the boys' situation.
2. Give other examples of natural objects (like the conch shell) that humans put to use.
3. How comfortable are you in the wilderness? If you have never been in the wilderness, what do you think it would be like to be there?

Imagine

1. Write a scene with a group of kids coming together for the first time in a strange situation.
2. Create a fictional character and describe his or her facial features in such a way that his or her personality is revealed.

Chapter 2

Comprehend

1. What is the function of the conch in the assembly?
2. Describe the attitudes of the different boys who speak during the assembly.
3. What do Ralph and Jack think of the island?
4. What is the boy with the mulberry-colored birthmark afraid of?
5. Why is Piggy upset at the scene of the signal fire?
6. What has presumably happened to the boy with the mulberry-colored birthmark at the end of the chapter?

Connect

1. Is the fear the littluns have of the "beastie" reasonable?
2. Compare what Ralph and Jack think about the little boy's dream of the snake-thing.
3. What changes and what stays consistent between the first assembly in Chapter 1 and the assembly in Chapter 2?

Extend

1. Have you ever done anything that you thought you could control, but that ended up getting out of your control?
2. What is the best way for children to make decisions in the absence of adults?
3. Find information from the library, the Internet, or your local fire station about what factors cause fire to spread and get out of control, and how to prevent it from happening.

Imagine

1. Write a short scene between two people in which one of the people is afraid of something and the other tries to convince her or him that there's nothing to be afraid of.

2. Sketch pictures of the faces of the main characters as you see them.

Chapter 3

Comprehend

1. What skills of the hunt does Jack demonstrate in the opening pages of this chapter?

2. Why is Ralph frustrated while building the shelters?

3. What separates Simon from the other boys?

4. Describe the relationship between Ralph and Jack.

Connect

1. Why is the signal fire important to Ralph but not as much to the other boys?

2. How has the society of the boys on the island developed? Who is serving what roles?

3. What connects Jack to the littluns?

Extend

1. Have you ever been afraid of something that you could not identify?

2. How do you proceed in situations with others when some group members do not pull their weight to get things done?

3. When you have conflict with someone, do you keep quiet or do you speak up?

Imagine

1. Imagine you are trying to hunt a wild pig. What skills would you need to have? Do some research, then write a short manual on how to hunt a pig.

2. How would you spend your time if you had to live on an island in the Pacific, and there was no existing society there?

Chapter 4

Comprehend

1. Summarize the first pages of the chapter describing the routines of the boys.

2. How does the coming of night affect the boys, especially the littluns?

3. What causes Ralph to tell Piggy to "shut up" (p. 70)?

4. What prevents Roger from throwing rocks that actually hit Henry?
5. How does the passing of the ship affect Simon?
6. What leads Jack to punch Piggy?

Connect

1. Describe how the older boys have changed since the beginning of the book.
2. How does the facial painting change Jack?
3. Why is meat so important to the boys? Is there symbolic meaning in the hunt, or in the meat itself?

Extend

1. What is the best way to react when someone is annoying to you?
2. Have you ever been tempted to do something wrong, but resisted the temptation? What kept you from doing the wrong thing?
3. How do you address violence between your peers? What can be done to prevent it?

Imagine

1. Rewrite the scene by the extinguished fire so that the boys reconcile their differences peacefully, with respect for each other.
2. Write a story with a character who wears a mask to hide his or her identity and then does things he or she would never do without the mask.

Chapter 5

Comprehend

1. What is Ralph worried about before the assembly? Why does he break into a trot when heading to the platform?
2. What does Ralph recognize of value in Piggy?
3. What rules does Ralph want to establish at the assembly?
4. How does Jack assert his rival authority and use the littluns' fear to his advantage?
5. What is Piggy's perspective on the assembly breaking apart?

Connect

1. How reasonable are Ralph's demands in the assembly?
2. How is the role of fear developing in the book?
3. What is it about adults that Ralph and the others feel that they need?

Extend

1. Do you or anyone you know believe in ghosts?

2. Based on your own experience, how do things "break apart" between groups of people?
3. Children play and adults work. Is it a good thing when children imitate adults through their play?

Imagine
1. Imagine yourself calling a meeting of your peers to discuss what is most important to you. If you had the authority to do so, and to establish rules for them, what rules would you establish?
2. Write a poem about fear and how it affects people.

Chapter 6

Comprehend
1. What is going on above the island at the beginning of the chapter?
2. How do the different boys react to Samneric's story of the beast?
3. What motivates the boys to visit the Castle Rock at the end of the island?
4. What causes Ralph's anger at the Castle Rock?

Connect
1. What does the dead parachutist symbolize?
2. What about the boys' behavior in this chapter is reasonable, and what about it is unreasonable?
3. How are the boys' attitudes about Ralph changing?
4. Has Ralph forgiven the boys for the missed rescue? Is he justified to blame them?

Extend
1. What causes people to make bad judgments for good reasons?
2. Describe a time when someone commanded you to do something that you thought was unreasonable.
3. What is the best balance between work and play for children?

Imagine
1. Write the dead parachutist's story.
2. Sketch a map of the island that includes the Castle Rock, or just illustrate the Castle Rock itself.

Chapter 7

Comprehend
1. What hinders the boys from climbing the mountain?
2. How does Ralph show bad judgment in this chapter?
3. What are Ralph's thoughts about Roger as they wait for Jack?

Connect
1. Why does Ralph ask Jack, "Why do you hate me?" (p. 134)?
2. What in the story so far would lead Jack to be jealous of Ralph's friendship with Piggy?
3. Why does Ralph grow nauseous when approaching the form on the mountain?

Extend
1. What is courage to you?
2. How do our perceptions shape our beliefs?

Imagine
1. Write a story that has a monster in it that turns out not to be a monster.

Chapter 8

Comprehend
1. Describe Jack's emotions during the assembly.
2. How does Jack portray Ralph during the assembly?
3. How does communal belief in the beast change the boys?
4. Why does Jack invite Ralph and Piggy to his feast?
5. What does Simon mean when he says, "What else is there to do?" (p. 146)?
6. What, in summary, is the message that the Lord of the Flies gives to Simon?

Connect
1. What role does fire play thus far in the book, and how does this chapter expand that role?
2. What is the significance of the savages saying, "The Chief has spoken" (p. 161)?
3. How is the boys' behavior in this chapter consistent with their previous behavior?
4. What does the Lord of the Flies symbolize?

Extend

1. If you were on the island at this point in the book, would you stay with Ralph or go with Jack?
2. How do we treat those in society who, like Simon, have different perspectives than most of us do?
3. List all the changes the boys have brought to the island during their time there.

Imagine

1. Imagine a demon or devil and write a conversation between yourself and that creature.
2. Write a story that features a storm that affects the events of the story.

Chapter 9

Comprehend

1. What motivates Simon to climb the mountain?
2. What motivates Ralph and Piggy to attend Jack's feast?
3. What motivates Simon to hurry to tell the boys what he has seen?
4. Describe the events that lead to Simon's death.
5. Do the boys realize that they are killing Simon? What evidence supports your answer?

Connect

1. What does pig's meat symbolize in the story? What does fruit symbolize?
2. What is the significance of flies in this chapter and the previous one?
3. How does the storm affect the events of this chapter?

Extend

1. Have you ever experienced a violent storm that led to disaster?
2. What other books or plays have you read that feature violent storms? How were the storms similar in how they affected the characters?
3. Is there ever a legitimate reason to take a life?

Imagine

1. Write a monologue for Simon if he had actually been able to tell the boys what he had seen. Include the reactions of the other boys.
2. Paint an abstract painting that depicts Simon's character. What colors best represent him? What colors represent the other characters?

Chapter 10

Comprehend
1. How is Ralph feeling about the events of the night before?
2. What are the excuses the different boys use to avoid taking responsibility for Simon's death?
3. How does Roger respond to the news that Wilfred will be beaten for no apparent reason?
4. What does it mean when Ralph hopes that "the beast would prefer lit-tluns" (p. 192)?
5. What happens during the attack? Why are Ralph and Eric both bruised?

Connect
1. What events earlier in the book indicate that Piggy would lose his glasses?
2. What events earlier in the book indicate that Ralph would lose his power?
3. Has Jack changed? If so, how? If not, why do you think he hasn't changed?

Extend
1. Are the boys still playing, as boys do? Is this just a game?
2. How do kids treat each other when adults are not around?
3. How realistic is the behavior of the boys on the island?

Imagine
1. Write a plot outline for how the boys could resolve their differences and still have fun on the island.
2. Write a song about Simon, perhaps a lament for him, or a song that tells his story.

Chapter 11

Comprehend
1. What problem does Ralph experience when he tries to think of what to do?
2. On page 198, Ralph remembers something that Simon said to him once, by the rocks. What did Simon say to him?
3. Why is Eric afraid of the savages' face paint (p. 199)?
4. What do Samneric discover about Ralph before they go to confront Jack and his tribe?
5. Why is the table rock in the ocean described as having the water "flower-ing" around it?

Connect
1. How has Roger changed throughout the course of the book?
2. What is symbolic about Piggy's name?
3. Compare the description of Piggy's death to the description of Simon's death.
4. How are the events of this scene inevitable? Or could they have been avoided?

Extend
1. What is preferable, adults' behavior or children's behavior?
2. Which human quality is stronger, logic or emotion? Why?
3. How does the scene of Piggy's murder affect you?

Imagine
1. Place Piggy in a situation where he would be respected and honored. What would the situation be, and what about Piggy would elevate him to the status of someone who is respected and honored?
2. Write a funeral eulogy for Piggy that reveals his character.

Chapter 12

Comprehend
1. Explain Ralph's reasons for returning to the Castle Rock after he wanders the island.
2. What does Ralph learn from Samneric?
3. What are the three choices Ralph has while trying to escape the savages?
4. What does Ralph realize about how the fire will affect Jack's tribe?
5. What is the attitude of the naval officer toward Ralph and the boys?
6. Why is the final image in the book of the navy ship?

Connect
1. How do the events of this chapter echo earlier events in the story?
2. How many boys on the island have died? How do we know?
3. Who is the darker character, Jack or Roger? Why?
4. Analyze the characters of Sam and Eric. How would you describe them and their role in the outcome of the story?

Extend
1. Assuming the naval ship did not arrive, what future would you predict for Jack's tribe?

2. How hopeful are you that children have the capacity to support each other and to get along? What is necessary for that to happen?

Imagine

1. Imagine the boys return to England and find that it has not been destroyed by war. Write a future path for each of the surviving major characters.
2. Write a song about *Lord of the Flies* that narrates the main events of the story but also carries an appropriate emotion.

Chapter Materials

Student Activity Sheet #18:
Conflict

Applicable Portion of the Novel: All

Objectives:
1. Students will trace major conflicts in *Lord of the Flies* from beginning to end.
2. Students will graphically represent conflict and articulate their understanding of how conflict affects action in the novel.

Common Core Standard(s): RL.9-10.3 and RL.9-10.10; RL.11-12.3 and RL.11-12.5

Directions: Choose a conflict in *Lord of the Flies* that interests you. Generate a visual representation of the conflict, tracing events in the novel that develop the conflict. Your visual representation may take the form of a timeline, a circle, a map, or any other form that best illustrates the conflict. For example, you can trace the conflict between Ralph and Jack by marking pivotal events in their encounters as spots on a game board. As a class, we will gather the list of conflicts you have generated and post the visual representations of those conflicts. We will discuss the conflict list and determine which conflicts have the most importance in the story.

Conflict: _____

Visual Representation:

Important developments in the conflict:

_____

_____

_____

_____

_____

Student Activity Sheet #19:
Plotline

Applicable Portion of the Novel: All

Objectives:
1. Students will track important events in *Lord of the Flies* through a visual plotline.
2. Students will connect plot to theme and use their understanding of what happens in the story to the story's overall meanings.

Common Core Standard(s): RL.9-10.5 and RL.9-10.10; RL.11-12.3, RL.11-12.5, and RL.11-12.10

Directions: A good way to keep on track with the plot is to develop a plotline, like a timeline of the story, with all events we know of added as they occur in the reading. Construct a plotline, like a timeline, either below or on a separate piece of paper. Include important events from the story. As we finish our first reading of the story, rank the plot events in order of importance. Compare your plotline with your conflict illustrations (see SAS #18) and look to see how your chosen conflict fits in with the overall plot. You may also connect the plotline with quotes from the Wall of Notable Quotes.

6

"If only they could get a message to us": Understanding and Writing About *Lord of the Flies*

Writing is an effective tool for learning (Applebee & Langer, 2011; Graham & Perin, 2007; Marzano, Pickering, & Pollock, 2001). Students engaged in writing practices from informal journaling to formally structured essays and test responses learn material with depth of understanding while furthering their own literacy. The literary analysis essay is the most common feature of rigorous high school English classes, and though the format of what we often call the "five-paragraph essay" has been critiqued (Pirie, 1998; Blau, 2003), the thesis/support/conclusion structure continues to dominate writing to assess literature unit goals (Applebee & Langer, 2011). Such writing is also required on the Advanced Placement (AP) examination in English Literature and Composition. But highly structured analytical essays are typically a summative expression of learning and, as such, constitute only a portion of the writing students may do while studying challenging works, such as *Lord of the Flies*. Students may write throughout their engagement with the novel, and I will present a number of strategies for making writing an effective tool for understanding (Murray, 2003).

What follows are innovative ways to introduce research-based writing techniques such as journaling, summary writing, and character analysis into your unit. Writing that addresses the Common Core State Standards' emphasis on citing textual evidence (RL.9-10.1) and understanding of informational texts (RI.9-10.1-6, 8) is also described. We will look specifically at AP examination writing prompts and discuss how you may use *Lord of the Flies* as a springboard for effective practice writing for the exam.

As stated in the course description for AP English Literature and Composition (College Board, 2010b),

Writing to understand a literary work may involve writing response and reaction papers along with annotation, freewriting, and keeping some form of a reading journal. Writing to explain a literary work involves analysis and interpretation, and may include writing brief, focused analyses on aspects of language and structure. Writing to evaluate a literary work involves making and explaining judgments about its artistry and exploring its underlying social and cultural values through analysis, interpretation, and argument. (p. 50)

These writing tasks described by College Board spring from the basic premise of literary study, which centers on reading experience, interpretation, and evaluation. One kind of topic students address in writing their AP essays, examples of which appear later in this chapter, calls upon students to produce an interpretation of a work in relation to a specific theme or literary element. The other kind of topic involves reading a passage from a work that may be unfamiliar (one poetry and one prose) and demonstrating the ability to arrive at an interpretation by activating good reading strategies, ranging from context clues to examination of imagery, structure, tone, or rhetorical devices (e.g., repetition, antithesis, reasoning models). Teaching literature at this level also means teaching students to construct written arguments that use specific evidence from the text and that stand up to close scrutiny.

Throughout this book, and especially in Chapters 4 and 5, I have presented topics for discussion and journal writing. Some of those topics are designed to enhance the reading experience, and many may be translated to formal, summative writing. By the time your students have read the book and reexamined it through the discussion and performance activities in Chapter 5, they may already have topics in mind for a summative essay. I encourage you to combine student-generated analytical writing topics with timed, on-demand essays from topics that you assign. Both practices will increase student competence in literary interpretation.

The following are writing activities I suggest to accompany your study of *Lord of the Flies*, moving from informal, low-stakes, writing-to-learn activities to formal AP examination formats. Finally, we will consider the many critical sources available to consult in developing and critiquing student interpretations of the book and entertain possible creative responses to the text.

Informal Response Writing

Informal response writing acknowledges that engagement with literature may involve emotional responses as well as intellectual ones (Rosenblatt, 1983). Whether using dialectical journals or learning logs (Gillespie, 2010), students can address global or local aspects of their reading in a nonthreatening way. Below are some typical prompts for informal responses prior to reading.

- Reflect on your experiences reading novels. Do you have a favorite?

- What do you know or what have you heard about *Lord of the Flies*?

- What are your greatest concerns about reading *Lord of the Flies*?

- What do you expect this experience reading *Lord of the Flies* to be like?

- What expectations do you have of yourself, and what do you expect from your teacher during this unit?

Before beginning their study of the text, students can also write in response to topics that relate to themes they will encounter in the novel, such as the following:

- Have you ever been in a situation that made you feel worried about your safety?

- How do you respond when someone you know is being picked on by others?

- How do you make decisions? Do you involve others or decide yourself?

- Is killing another human being ever justified? If so, under what circumstances?

- Do you believe in the supernatural? How easy is it for you to suspend disbelief when you see supernatural elements in TV shows or movies?

Discussion topics from Chapter 5 may also work for this journal. You can certainly generate your own prereading topics, but any of these can get students thinking about the imaginative world they are about to enter as they read *Lord of the Flies*.

Once students have begun reading, you will want them to continue writing informal responses, questions, and comments as they work through the text. This journal writing can reflect on the story and the process of reading it. Journals may be kept by individual students or may be done as blogs or online discussion boards, making them a community enterprise. Encourage students to have a writing journal or computer screen available *as* they read, so that they can write down questions, concerns, or insights they have as those questions, concerns, or insights arise. If students have their own copies of the novel that they can write in, all the better, as you can teach them to make marginal notes in the text.

There's a good deal of freedom in response-based writing, and you can learn about what your students notice in their reading that spurs their writing. One student may write about the characters almost exclusively, whereas another may focus primarily on his or her frustration with the difficulty of the narrative descriptions, and another may choose to imagine herself in that situation. Personal reactions, feelings, and progressions of feelings are valid as well.

Ongoing Journal

Throughout Chapter 4 of this book, Discussion/Journal topics were proposed in connection with an initial reading of *Lord of the Flies*. Here are more ideas that may help students generate writing as they work through the text from the beginning to the end:

- Have students keep track of *how* they read the novel. For example, how much they read alone, how much they read in class with classmates, and how much they read aloud. Have them log how much time they spend reading during each sitting and gauge (on a scale of 1–10) how difficult the reading is. They may note whether they get tired before they stop or whether they feel they could go on further than what was assigned.

- Have students write how they feel while reading, what their involvement with the various characters is, and what they think the story is about. If their thoughts change as they progress through the novel, have them note it in their journals.

- Have students try to make connections between what is happening in the novel and experiences they have heard of or experienced themselves. They can also write about examples from popular culture that the story reminds them of, or to write about what makes the story different from what they have experienced.

- Have students write a journal of one of the characters, such as Jack, Ralph or Piggy, writing as that character and reflecting on that character's feelings and thoughts about what is happening on the island.

- Have students write about themselves and, specifically, their own sense of self, as reflected in the story. What qualities of different characters do they see in themselves? What qualities do they lack but admire? What qualities are they glad they do not possess? These inquiries into self can increase students' interest in the plot of the story.

I would strongly encourage pre- and postdiscussion writing as a way to help students prepare for discussions, retain what they heard and said during discussion, and exercise a form of metacognition. Students can use these informal writings as a way to track their own understanding of the text and identify personal breakthroughs during the process of reading and interpreting.

Journal writing often leads students to good ideas for more formal writing that they do, or good ideas for inquiry projects (see Chapter 7 of this book). The digital format may align informal class writing with students' already-established literacy practices (Buck, 2012). In *The Digital Writing Workshop* (2009), Troy Hicks demonstrated how students can build online learning communities related to their reading with blogs, wikis, or other social networking software. Students can start homepages for characters, share their thoughts as they read in a reviewable version of their reading journals, or collaborate in building commentary on the action.

Writing About Character: Intervention

As students develop their understanding of the different characters and how they interact with one another, they may see spots in the novel where characters make poor decisions that could have been avoided if the character had someone to consult with. The character intervention writing activity (see page 152) operates on the premise that students can imagine themselves taking a character aside and talking to the character before an important event, or during a critical time, and giving that character advice to save him from harm, or from harming others.

Students can do these character intervention scripts during their first reading or as review. Beyond the character charts, the joint International Reading Association/National Council of Teachers of English (IRA/NCTE) website ReadWriteThink (http://www.readwritethink.org) offers many visual thinking tools that can help students keep track of their growing understanding, and character maps are just one option (for more possibilities, see http://www.readwritethink.org/materials/dramamap).

Summary Writing: News Report

According to a research report to the Carnegie Corporation (Graham & Perin, 2007), summarization is the second-most effective type of writing instruction for improving writing among middle and high school students, and that assertion echoes an earlier meta-analysis by Marzano, Pickering, and Pollock (2001) that ranked summary writing and note taking second among teaching strategies that had the most impact on student learning across disciplines. One way to combine the rigor required by summary writing with technology and collaboration is to have students develop online, interactive news reports for the events of the novel (see page 153).

Casting summary writing in the format of a news story allows students to take on a voice that may not be their own, which takes pressure off of them to

ACTIVITY (SAS #20): CHARACTER INTERVENTION

One activity that focuses on character and can introduce elements of psychological theory is something that I call "character intervention." As students read the novel, have them develop profiles of different characters using terms that translate easily to character analysis (see the character charts from SAS #8 in Chapter 4 of this book). For example, students can use the categories in the chart (positive traits, negative traits, motivations, fears), along with indications of which characters demonstrate each behavior, to better understand the characters on a psychological level. You will notice that the designations of traits, motivations, and fears are judgments on the character, and the "demonstrated by" prompt that goes with those judgments requires specific reference to character words or actions. Using the charts and any other notes they have taken during reading, students can construct visual character diagnosis sheets with categories such as *biggest mistake*, *next likely move*, *potential protector(s)*, and *potential aggressor(s)*. Anticipating problems on the horizon for that character, students then write a summary, framed as a speech to be delivered at an "intervention" for that character. Have students identify the point in the novel where they would have the intervention for the character in order to prevent disaster. For example, an intervention with Roger may happen right before he rolls the rock onto Piggy, or perhaps earlier, when he is throwing rocks around Henry. With the character intervention script, your students will engage in the kind of character analysis we would typically expect in analytical writing, but the context of the intervention will frame the task in a way that motivates students. Students can even act out their intervention scripts or read them to the class.

Here is an example of a character intervention with Simon that could take place during Chapter 9 of the novel:

Simon,

I'm worried about you, and we need to talk right away. You showed great bravery by climbing the mountain, especially after that frightening interview with the pig's head, talking to you as though it were the Lord of the Flies. You have shown kindness to all you meet, especially Ralph, and you've tolerated the littluns as they follow you around. Most of all, you overcame your own disgust and vomiting to help untangle the poor, dead airman. I know you want to tell the others right away, but you might consider waiting until the storm passes. Jack and the others have shown little restraint when they have fresh meat to eat, and they may not recognize you if you come upon them suddenly . . .

ACTIVITY (SAS #21): INTERACTIVE NEWS REPORT

One interactive way to have students write summaries that get them to delve deeper than mere plot summary is to have students write news reports of the events of the novel, together with associated feature stories. Using the journalistic questions of what, who, when, where, how, and why, students can generate leads and stories that they present to their classmates in an online format. If your school does not have its own online course management format, you can use Google Groups or Blogger or any other freely available online format. Just as readers can respond to news stories in *The New York Times*, MSNBC, or other major news organizations, so your students can add blog-like comments in response to the news stories posted, making the experience of writing about *Lord of the Flies* akin to witnessing an ongoing news event. The comments on the news stories serve to extend the consideration of the events described into analysis and criticism. The following is an example news story created from the events of Chapter 4.

News Headline: Ship Passes Island Unnoticed
Subheading: Signal Fire Allowed to Go Cold at Critical Time

Several boys on the island noticed a ship passing on the horizon today, and in a stunning revelation, they found that the signal fire was allowed to go cold so that the assigned attendants of the fire could join in a pig hunt. Ralph, the chief of the tribe, and several others raced to try to revive the fire but arrived too late. The ship passed on without noticing that the boys were on the island. Jack and his hunters, including Samneric, who were assigned to keep the fire going, returned to the scene of the fire with their first kill, a young pig. A loud confrontation between Ralph and Jack ensued, and when Piggy accused Jack of irresponsible behavior, Jack assaulted him and broke his glasses. Word is that a feast of pig followed, but we will have more details as they are made available to us.

Post comments on this story:
1. t.g.: It's a classic battle between the hunters and the domestic types.
2. g.c.: Piggy needs to learn not to confront Jack. He's a madman.
3. b.l.: I heard that Simon was crying, and that he offered his meat to Piggy at the feast.
4. z.d.: Would the ship have seen the fire anyway? Ralph should let it go.

write in a stiff, academic voice that is unconvincing. Students can videotape their news reports and post them for their classmates to see. Sharing responsibility for "reporting," students can track stories as they work through the novel, and you can assign different students or groups of students to produce the stories or summaries.

Other Literary Elements

Beyond character, all of the traditional literary elements may become starting points for writing about *Lord of the Flies*. The discussion sections from Chapter 5 related to setting, conflict, plot, point of view, symbol, and theme may be helpful in establishing these starting points, and we will consider how the AP prompts often make use of stock literary elements for timed essays. What is essential to this approach is that we focus less on the definition of the literary element as an end in itself, and more on the need for students to be able to operationalize their understanding of literary terms and internalize that understanding for later use.

ACTIVITY (SAS #22): TITLE DEFENSE

Lord of the Flies offers us an opportunity to examine how a book's title reflects the content, and how a title can be appropriate or inappropriate as a lure to potential readers. This activity, which I call "title defense," asks students to consider titles that were proposed for Golding's book, either by the author himself or by his editors, and that were rejected (Carey, 2009). Students are to rank them, then argue as to which is the best to use, as though they were part of the editorial process of choosing a title. Whether you structure this as an informal journal, a timed practice essay, or an exam question is up to you, but you may also find that the activity can produce good debate in discussion. Writing will force students to think about theme in the book, but also to think critically on a broader scale about the function that labels, titles, and brands play for consumers.

Here are titles that were considered and rejected, according to John Carey in his 2009 biography of Golding:

- Strangers from Within
- A Cry of Children
- Nightmare Island
- This Island's Mine
- Beast in the Jungle
- An Island of Their Own
- Fun and Games
- The Isle Is Full of Noises

⚘ To End an Island

Once students have had a chance to argue the effectiveness of the different titles, they may discuss why they think *Lord of the Flies*, suggested by an editor at Faber and Faber named Alan Pringle (Carey, 2009, p. 161), was chosen as the title, and whether that was a good choice, given the events, themes, and outcome of the novel.

ACTIVITY (SAS #23):
POINTING AND WRITING FROM A LINE

This writing activity builds on the Wall of Notable Quotes (see Chapter 4, SAS #6) and uses elements of Blau's literature workshop approach (2003). The activity is called "pointing." As students read the novel, have them keep a list in their journals of individual lines from the book that they find memorable. This could be because the line stands out as emblematic of the book's themes, offers insight of some kind, or is confusing and needs further illumination. Students are encouraged to write lines on the Wall of Notable Quotes, which is either posted on the wall of the classroom or as part of an electronic bulletin board. The list will be available as a reference for discussion and writing.

When students have finished the initial read-through and are working to develop interpretations, have them access their list of favorite lines, and then introduce the activity by saying that the class is going to "reread the novel in 3 minutes." The way that you will reread the novel will be to do a choral reading of favorite lines that students have selected. The rules will be simple:

1. Nobody owns a line, so if two people want to read the same line, they can.
2. Students may repeat their lines out loud as many times as they want.
3. Only one voice at a time, so if two students start to read at the same time, one stops and waits until the other has finished.
4. It does not matter where in the book the line appears, beginning to end. They don't have to be read in order.
5. The reading goes on until the teacher calls for a stop.

It is a good idea if you start with one of your favorite lines, then wait until a student jumps in. What will follow will be poetic and fun, with students bringing up lines that others had perhaps forgotten about. Imagine, for example, hearing this succession of lines:

"Why do you hate me?"
"He looked for understanding and found only respect."
"Jack!"

"The hunters followed, wedded to her in lust"

"But s'pose they don't make sense? Not here, on this island?"

"A murmur, almost a moan, rose and passed away."

"I've got the conch!"

"Darkness poured out."

"A littlun was talking in his sleep."

"The luminous flowering around the rock."

"The true, wise friend called Piggy . . . "

"Kill the beast! Cut his throat! Spill his blood!"

"Why do you hate me?"

"I've got the conch!"

"I think we ought to climb the mountain."

"Smoke!"

After you let the reading go on for a while, stop it before it runs out of steam, so that students are left wanting to hear more. Have them journal immediately after the activity, citing lines they heard that they found interesting or that they had forgotten about. Then have them choose one line from their own list or from the reading, put it at the top of a page, and write about the novel using that line as a starting point. As they write, they may bring in any of the other lines they wrote down or heard to support what they have to say about the book. Thus, they will be writing from evidence or specifics in the text to build interpretation, rather than starting with their interpretation and then searching the text for evidence. This activity therefore reverses a typical progression of thinking and helps students to consider the evidence first. A good progression from this writing is to break students into groups of three and have them share their chosen lines and writing. Students discuss their interpretations and then share out to the larger group, either nominating themselves or someone from their group to share. This process provides great prewriting for more formal analysis.

You may notice in the example lines above that some of the lines come from characters and some come from the narrator. Another variation of this pointing approach to writing about the text is for you or your students to list quotes (such as the lines above), then have students identify the speaker (even if the speaker is the narrator) and tell where in the story the speaker says this line, and what the line reveals about the character and the story. You may pull quotes yourself or use the Wall of Notable Quotes for material. Either way, the value of these activities is that they are relatively low stakes, yet they focus students on the relationship between evidence and interpretation. The reading aloud of lines from the text may even sound poetic, which is a bonus.

Screen Adaptations: Movie Reviews

Two full-length feature films have been made from this book. The first, directed by Peter Brook (1963), is shot in black and white and remains faithful to the text in detail. The film is available in many public libraries and is on YouTube in 10 segments of approximately 10 minutes each, which makes for good use in the classroom.

The second film, directed by Harry Hook (1990), Americanizes the tale, featuring a group of boys from a sort of JROTC school, and the film is noticeably removed from a WWII era. While the film strays considerably from the book in the way it embodies the beast and other details (including a wounded pilot who eventually becomes the beast), it does essentially follow the plot of the novel, including the deaths of Simon and Piggy and the arrival of a bewildered military officer.

While I do not generally recommend viewing entire films in the classroom unless you have objectives related to learning how to view film as an art form (see Golden, 2001), these films based on *Lord of the Flies* provide great material for critical review, as students can evaluate the directors' visions in view of their own interpretations of the novel.

Advanced Placement Essay Free-Response Topic Formats

On the AP exam, students complete a series of multiple-choice questions in connection with reading passages, followed by three 40-minute written responses, called free-response questions. These free-response questions on poetry, fiction, and drama come in two basic forms. The first two responses on the exam challenge students to analyze authorial technique based on a specific literary passage (one poetry and one prose), requiring on-the-spot close reading and interpretation. I will refer to these as "passage-based," conflating the poetry and prose topics into one discussion. The third topic on the exam, sometimes referred to as the "open" topic, poses a challenge of theme, literary device, or interpretation and then lets students choose which work they wish to write about in connection with the prompt. Some of these open topics identify a theme and then ask the student to address the theme as it is presented in the work they choose. Other open topics present an interpretation from a secondary source, either commenting on a single work or on a certain type of work, and then ask students to write about how that interpretation may be applied to a work of their choosing (see the Introducing Critical Sources section later in this chapter). Both variations of the open topic offer a list of works from which to choose, but allow students to use nonlisted works if they have literary merit. Below are examples and discussions of both the passage-based free-response topics and the open topics.

Passage-Based Free-Response Topics

The passage-based topics require students to analyze a passage of poetry or prose and discuss it in relation to some type of literary technique. Authorial intent is implied in these topics, as the techniques that are mentioned are typically methods that authors would not arrive at haphazardly. For example, one topic from 2005 paired two poems by William Blake and asked students to "compare and contrast the two poems, taking into consideration the poetic techniques Blake uses in each" (College Board, 2005a, p. 2). Poetic techniques are not specified here, but in another topic related to a passage of narrative, "characterization" is used to reflect the narrator's attitude and writers are told to consider "diction, tone, detail, and syntax" (College Board, 2005b, p. 2). Yet another topic asks the writers to "write an essay in which you show how the author uses literary devices to achieve her purpose" (College Board, 2005a, p. 3). Indeed, imagery, tone, syntax, structure, and other literary devices commonly come up in these topics.

Open Free-Response Topics

Here are some example open topics that have been released by College Board. I have chosen these because they lend themselves to allowing students to use *Lord of the Flies* as the applicable text.

- *From 2005*—One of the strongest human drives seems to be a desire for power. Write an essay in which you discuss how a character in a novel or a drama struggles to free himself or herself from the power of others or seeks to gain power over others. Be sure to demonstrate in your essay how the author uses this power struggle to enhance the meaning of the work. (College Board, 2005b, p. 4)

- *From 2009*—Many works of literature deal with political or social issues. Choose a novel or play that focuses on a political or social issue. Then write an essay in which you analyze how the author uses literary elements to explore this issue and explain how the issue contributes to the meaning of the work as a whole. Do not merely summarize the plot. (College Board, 2009, p. 4)

- *From 2010*—The British novelist Fay Wheldon offers this observation about happy endings: "The writers, I do believe, who get the best and most lasting response from readers are the writers who offer a happy ending through moral development. By a happy ending, I do not mean mere fortunate events—a marriage or a last-minute rescue from death—but

Activity (SAS #24): Sample Free-Response

One way you can help your students prepare for these passage-based AP examination questions is to use the sample questions provided by College Board, then take a piece of text from *Lord of the Flies* and substitute it for the passage that originally appeared. You may need to change the wording of the question to accommodate the substitution, but you will have something that your students can use for practice. Another option is to create your own original topics using passages from the novel, modeling them on those that appear on the exams. Below is one example of a passage-based topic I created for *Lord of the Flies*, which is reprinted on SAS #24.

Directions: In the following passage from *Lord of the Flies*, Simon awakes to find that he has had a fainting spell. In a well-written essay, explain how the author uses imagery to convey tone and reveal Simon's character.

> With the running of the blood Simon's fit passed into the weariness of sleep. He lay in the mat of creepers while the evening advanced and the cannon continued to play. At last he woke and saw dimly the dark earth close by his cheek. Still he did not move, but lay there, his face sideways on the earth, his eyes looking dully before him. Then he turned over, drew his feet under him and laid hold of the creepers to pull himself up. When the creepers shook the flies exploded from the guts with a vicious note and clamped back on again. Simon got to his feet. The light was unearthly. The Lord of the Flies hung on his stick like a black ball.
> Simon spoke aloud to the clearing.
> "What else is there to do?"
> Nothing replied. Simon turned away from the open space and crawled through the creepers till he was in the dusk of the forest. He walked drearily between the trunks, his face empty of expression and the blood was dry round his mouth and chin. Only sometimes as he lifted the ropes of creeper aside and chose his direction from the trend of the land, he mouthed words that did not reach the air.
> Presently the creepers festooned the trees less frequently and there was a scatter of pearly light from the sky down through the trees. This was the backbone of the island, the slightly higher land that lay beneath the mountain where the forest was no longer deep jungle. Here there were wide spaces interspersed with thickets and huge trees and the trend of the ground led him up as the forest opened. He pushed on, staggering sometimes with his weariness but never stopping. The usual brightness was gone from his eyes and he walked with a sort of glum determination like an old man. (p. 166-167)

some kind of spiritual reassessment or moral reconciliation, even with the self, even at death." Choose a novel or play that has the kind of ending Wheldon describes. In a well-written essay, identify the "spiritual reassessment or moral reconciliation" evident in the ending and explain its significance in the work as a whole. You may select work from the list below or another novel or play of literary merit. (College Board, 2010, p. 76)

From 2012—"And after all, our surroundings influence our lives and characters as much as fate, destiny or any supernatural agency"—Pauline Hopkins, *Contending Forces*. Choose a novel or play in which cultural, physical, or geographical surroundings shape psychological or moral traits in a character. Then write a well-organized essay in which you analyze how surroundings affect this character and illuminate the meaning of the work as a whole. (College Board, 2012, p. 4)

ACTIVITY (SAS #25): AP FREE-RESPONSE TOPICS

Give students the sample open free-response questions above and have them use *Lord of the Flies* to address the questions. Giving students opportunities to write these types of analysis both in timed and untimed settings will be valuable. Topics are printed on SAS #25 at the back of this chapter.

On their faces, each of these open free-response prompts offers students the opportunity to write lucidly about *Lord of the Flies*. Discuss with your students how they might approach writing a 40-minute response to these topics. Of help to them will be an understanding of the logic behind the structure of the open free-response questions themselves. What is vital to our discussion of the first topic is the idea of identifying a theme or issue common to human society—in this case, "power"—and applying it to logical, supported written argument. What the topic tells us is that something is true: "One of the strongest human drives *seems to be* a desire for power" (College Board, 2005b, p. 4, itals. mine). What the examiners are asking students to do is to accept the premise of the statement first, and then, having accepted the premise, apply it to a literary work. Students have the flexibility either to write about the will to escape the power of others, which is essentially to write about the theme of oppression from the point of view of the oppressed, or to write about the desire of one character or another to gain power, which is closer to the premise as laid out and more applicable to *Lord of the Flies*.

The essence of the final statement in the topic, however, which is common to all topics listed here and nearly all free-response topics, is the connection between either theme or authorial technique and the meaning of the entire work. The topic tells us to show "how the author uses this power struggle *to enhance the meaning of the work*" (College Board, 2005b, p. 4, itals. mine). Implied in that statement is another premise: that the literary work has a singularly definable meaning, and that the theme of power is "used" to "enhance" that meaning, rather than constituting meaning itself. Theme is connected to technique, which reveals meaning. Looking at the open free-response topic from 2009, we see nearly the exact same wording: "explain how the issue contributes to the meaning of the work *as a whole*" (College Board, 2009, p. 4, itals mine). If nothing else, be sure to tell your students to read all parts of the topic they are addressing.

What teachers can take out of this discussion of the open free-response topics is that the theme or element described will be a common characteristic of great literature, such as unconventional characters, power struggles, important events, or physical journeys, and that the writer will be required to connect the theme or element specifically to the meaning of the entire work. Detailed references to the work and an understanding of the way a work develops its meaning will be essential.

More Test Advice

In their guide to preparing to write for AP topics, College Board emphasized four key guidelines (College Board, 2011b, p. 1):
1. Take time to organize your ideas.
2. Make pertinent use of the text given to you to analyze.
3. Quote judiciously from it to support your observations.
4. Be logical in your exposition of ideas.

Writers are encouraged to use the vocabulary of the field, which runs the gamut from specific rhetorical devices (allusion, syllogism) to broad concerns (ideology, persuasion). The formula is simple on its face: Form a logical thought about the work and lay it out so that a reader can understand it, supporting it with direct evidence from the work. The other key is to know your literary devices. Beyond practicing with model topics, engaging in activities centered on literary elements, such as those above and in Chapter 5 of this book, will help students prepare for success.

Once your students have an investment in taking the AP exam, have them develop their expertise by creating a poster of "advice" for taking the AP exam in English Literature and Composition. Students can also create or draft an oral or written defense of example AP exam essays they have written on *Lord of the Flies*, arguing that they deserve a certain score based upon merits and College Board 9-point rubric. These kinds of activities will make test prep less monotonous.

Critical Analysis and Making Connections

Judith Langer's study *Beating the Odds: Teaching Middle and High School Students to Read and Write Well* (2000) showed conclusively that teachers who achieve the best results in student reading and writing performance are those who are willing to go beyond reaching their simple comprehension goals and make connections between the literary works and students' lives, broader contexts, and other subjects. Such connection building fits the final realm of the AP course description that leads to critical writing on a work of literature. College Board's description of the writing required in college writing courses reads, "Writing to evaluate a literary work involves making and explaining judgments about its artistry and exploring its underlying social and cultural values through analysis, interpretation, and argument" (College Board, 2011a, p. 1). This type of critical analysis and writing represents the most complex and challenging task associated with studying literature, as it asks us to make value judgments on material that we may feel we have no right to judge. But we must, and engaging in that process leads students to enter conversations with the great thinkers of the past and present, as we compare Golding's work to say, Swift's *Gulliver's Travels* (Reilly, 1992) or *The Bacchae* of Euripides (Baker, 1963).

While the topics for the free-response essays on the AP exam often ask students to relate specific authorial technique to the meaning of the work as a whole, meaning is something arrived at referentially, through comparison between the world of the literary work and the frame of reference of the reader. In order to get students to reach this point of critical examination of text, we must give them opportunities to forge connections between the world of the novel and social or political worlds of today.

Through the processes of reading, responding, discussing, and listening, students may develop perspectives that they would be more likely to share with their peers outside of class than in class. Perhaps a student reader sees the text as representative of the power struggles typical in any hierarchical institution, such as families, schools, and communities. Perhaps another student sees the novel as representing aggression caused by repressed male-to-male attraction. These and hundreds of other thoughts about the novel can be defended with "logical exposition of ideas" and "judicious" use of quotes (College Board, 2011b. p. 1). But beyond strict analysis, these perceptions take the work of literature beyond itself and into the broader world of ideas. If we think of the novel as representative of power struggles in institutions, we must look to both the novel and the world in order to explain our ideas. We start to make value judgments of the work as an expression of those ideas. We criticize.

ACTIVITY (SAS #26): NOTES, NOTES, NOTES

Have students look at all of the notes and journal entries they have written in the process of reading and discussing *Lord of the Flies*, then ask them to draw some conclusions about the text. Have them consult their notes for thoughts and impressions that will lead to thesis statements about the novel. Have them write a short critical essay on some aspect of the text that they choose, evaluating its relevance or connection to contemporary culture.

Another way to approach critical perspectives as a tool for understanding and writing about *Lord of the Flies* is to apply recognized critical lenses to the novel and then to see how those lenses shape our interpretation (Appleman, 2009; Gillespie, 2010). We can begin these forays into the world of critical theory by asking broad questions that encourage students to look at the text through the lenses we wish to employ. For example, we might ask one of these questions:

1. How does the all-male cast influence the events of *Lord of the Flies*? What clues to an attitude about feminine energy are given, especially in the killing of the sow?
2. How does the division of labor on the island determine privilege and power?
3. Where is the moral center of this text? Is it represented in one character or is moral norming shared? What opposing forces shape the boys behavior?
4. How does Simon represent a savior figure? Is he effective in that role?
5. What historical influences are evident in Golding's novel?

These are just a few examples of questions that can lead to reading and writing focused by different critical lenses. Such questions can be laid out for inquiry before students enter the text of after they have completed their own reading. You and your students can create questions of your own that reflect student interests. Gillespie (2010), in his book *Doing Critical Theory*, offered a companion CD with short explanations of different critical theories that can be handed out to students to inform their inquiry.

Other questions that relate to critical perspectives will require students to examine primary or secondary critical sources. For example, you may ask the question, "How does this novel reflect Freudian concepts of the Id, the Ego, and the Superego?" Students can read Freud, Marx, or any other major thinker and then look for parallels that illuminate the novel. Although examining primary sources challenges students and broadens their perspectives through recognition of allusions and influences, secondary sources in the form of historical or contemporary written criticism of *Lord of the Flies* offer similar opportunities to deepen understanding.

Introducing Critical Sources

When students have exhausted their own resources and energy in building their individual readings of the novel, they will be ready to join the larger conversations about *Lord of the Flies* by reading published commentary and criticism. I have mentioned earlier in this book that I encourage teachers to avoid frontloading students' experience with *Lord of the Flies* by bogging them down in criticism prior to their first reading. But by the time they have read, analyzed, discussed, written about, and criticized the text, they will be ready to join the critical conversation that has been going on since the novel was first published in 1954.

As their teacher and tour guide, you will have the responsibility of bringing your students into the discussion in a way that does not overwhelm them, yet challenges their thinking. Knowing something of what the conversation about *Lord of the Flies* has been will allow you to be that guide, given the time you have.

As mentioned in the section on the AP examination topics, some open free-response questions present an interpretation from a secondary source and then ask students to write from that source. You may prepare your students for this type of topic by consulting a handful of critical essays on *Lord of the Flies,* pulling short excerpts that demonstrate a major point in the essay, and asking students to either accept the premise and defend it in writing or reject it, similarly defending the rejection. Below are several examples, with the sources from which they came:

> As a social allegory of human regression the novel is more easily (perhaps too neatly) explainable as "the way in which, when the civilized restraints which we impose on ourselves are abandoned, the passions of anger, lust, and fear wash across the mind, obliterating commonsense and care, and life once again becomes nasty, brutish and short."
> —B. S. Oldsey and S. Weintraub (1965, pp. 29–30), with quote from J. Bowen (1959)

> The rebirth of evil is made certain by the fatal defects inherent in human nature, and the haunted island we occupy must always be a fortress on which enchanted hunters pursue the beast. There is no rescue. The making of history and the making of myth are finally the selfsame process—an old one in which the soul makes its own place, its own reality.
> —J. R. Baker (1963, p. 29)

If we respond to what is on the page we shall find in the novel less the pummeling of humanism than the growth in stature, in credibly boyish terms, of the "true wise friend" who on the last page is almost the tragic hero. Like the other characters Piggy does embody meaning of various kinds, so that we become aware through our imaginative response to the boy of wider horizons and deeper problems beyond him. On the other hand, he is too diminutive to support an acceptable representative significance, just as Jack cannot be Satan or the Power Urge, though he may reveal truths about both to us, and Simon is both less and more than the Saint.

—M. Kinkead-Weekes & I. Gregor (1967, p. 20)

The pig-hunting of former days has been relatively innocent, but to fully dramatize the deep inner evil that takes possession of the boys after they accept the Beast as their god, Golding depicts more than a mere killing. Conjuring up the most shocking imagery he could use to show the degeneration of these preadolescents, he describes the slaughter of a mother sow in terms of a sexual assault. How better to portray the children's loss of innocence (since children are no strangers to killing) than by picturing them as perpetrators of an Oedipal violation? The vividness of this scene makes it both a powerfully realistic component of the essential story and a major contribution to the novel's symbolic scheme.

—A. Johnston (1980, pp. 12–13)

Simon and Piggy are, indeed, alike in sharing a role in *Lord of the Flies*, the role of outsider, scapegoat, and victim of murder. Though the two are alike in this way, however, they are otherwise very different from one another and represent, indeed, two mighty opposites, two warring ways of looking at the world.... Faith in science and rationality, with a marked disbelief in anything supernatural, is characteristic of Piggy. Simon, by contrast, is intuitive, introspective, other-worldly; his central insight is gained in a vision or trance; Simon represents and has access to a dimension of experience it is proper to call religious. Piggy cannot understand Simon and thinks him mad.

—S. J. Boyd (1988, p. 15)

Water and rocks, ebb and flow, angles and circles, microcosm and macrocosm, reason and intuition, good and evil, flies and butterflies: rhythm beats in *Lord of the Flies*, sometimes loud, sometimes with "an undertone less perceptive than the susurration of the blood," but always with the regularity of waves against the reef. This continual back-and-forth motion, the rhythm of life, is complemented by a rhythmic use of gradation suggesting the constant progress of evil. The killing of pigs and the throwing of rocks, two important activities of the boys on the island, provide a metaphorical structure for the illustration of the author's theme . . .

. . . By introducing correspondences between setting and characters Golding intimates that the same law governs the geophysical world and the world of man. Human nature is an aspect of nature at large. Man is neither worse nor better than nature; the same evil principle permeates and harms both.

—J. Delbaere-Garant (1978, pp. 72, 76)

Golding's own comments about *Lord of the Flies* continually focus on the potentials and the limitations of the democratic ideal. Though he supports a democratic doctrine, he recognizes its weaknesses: "You can't give people freedom without weakening society as an implement of war, if you like, and so this is very much like sheep among wolves. It's not a question with me as to whether democracy is the right way so much as to whether democracy can survive and remain what it is." By giving up all its principles, the island society of *Lord of the Flies* demonstrates the inefficacy of political organizations that attempt to check human beings' worst destructive instincts. It is only by first recognizing these dark powers that democracy can hope to control them.

—L. L. Dickson (1990, p. 25)

The boys play at controlling sea creatures and each other, and the naval officer who lands on the island to recue the boys at first interprets their hunt for Ralph as an ordinary children's game. This introduces an entirely new level of complexity into an already many-layered novel. Is the whole thing a game or not, the natural behavior of humankind (including children) or an imitation of the adult world? . . .

. . . The conch is not a symbol of authority but a boy's toy version of a symbol of authority, serving the same purpose as a toy telephone. Until the arrival of the navy, there is no voice at the other end of the line. By the same token, the voting for chief, Ralph's authority, the hunt, the kill, and the feast each follow the pattern of child's play, as the boys imitate what their elders might do in similar circumstances. Each chapter reveals a new game or a new stage of the game.

—K. Olsen (2000, pp. 20–21)

There are no excuses for complacency in the fretful conscientiousness of Ralph, the leader, nor in Piggy's anxious commonsense, nor are the miscreants made to seem exceptional. When he first encounters a pig Jack Merridew is quite incapable of harming it, "because of the enormity of the knife descending and cutting into living flesh," and even the delinquent Roger is at first restrained by the taboos of "parents and school and policemen and the law." Strip these away and even Ralph might be a hunter; it is his duties as a leader that save him, rather than any intrinsic virtue in himself. Like any orthodox moralist Golding insists that Man is a fallen creature, but he refuses to hypostatize Evil or to locate it in a dimension of its own. On the contrary Beelzebub, Lord of the Flies, is Roger and Jack and you and I, ready to declare himself as soon as we permit him to.

—J. Peter (1957, pp. 252–253)

The ritual murder of Simon is as ironic as it is inevitable. Ironically, he is killed as the beast before he can explain that the beast does not exist. His horrid death refutes his aborted revelation: the beast exists, all right, not where we thought to find it, but within ourselves. Inevitably, we kill our savior who "would set us free from the repetitious nightmare of history." Unable to perceive his truth, we huddle together in the circle of our fear and reenact his ritual murder, as ancient as human history itself. Golding's murderous boys, the products of centuries of Christianity and Western civilization, explode the hope of Christ's sacrifice by repeating the pattern of his crucifixion. Simon's fate underlines the most awful truths about human nature: its blindness, its irrationality, its blood lust.

—L. S. Friedman (1993, p. 25), with quote from J. R. Baker (1965)

An uninhabited island, the setting for this story, contains at least two vying elements—the symbolic system and the symbol-destroying force. These two elements, juxtaposed and intertwined with each other, are inherent to the topography, scenery, and various aspects of the island, interacting in a delicate balance, out of which comes the endlessly multi-vocal differentiated world. The conch is a typical example of this sort of balance. Lack of this balance brings about the world of non-differentiation, uniformity, and violence. The symbolic system is first introduced into the island by a group of boys who become united under the rules of the conch. In disregard of its natural shape, which keeps the delicate balance between the symbolic system and the symbol-destroying force, the boys confine the function of the conch strictly to a univocal, fixed sign. The destructive power, suppressed under the control of the univocal sign, gathers its strength in the boys' subconscious and is actualized in mob violence.

—Y. Sugimura (2008, p. 15)

In *Lord of the Flies* the ideographic structure consists in two movements; in the first, the story is seen from the point of view of the childish protagonist, Ralph, as he gradually grows more and more aware of the island's disintegration. In the second movement, the coda which concludes the fable, we see events from a new point of view, that of the adult naval officer, who is completely unaware and largely indifferent to the suffering. The coda, in conjunction with such symbols as the parachutist, indicates that adulthood is also inadequate to prevent destruction.

—V. Tiger (1974, p. 52)

James Gindin insists that Golding's description of Jack's gang—who are English—"deliberately suggests the Nazis." Despite a preference for the universal aspects of Golding's fiction, Leighton Hodson suggests Piggy might represent the "democrat and intellectual," Jack "Hitler," and Roger a "potential concentration camp guard." L. L. Dickson identifies the novel as political allegory, referring to World War II atrocities, particularly those inflicted upon the Jews. Suzie Mackenzie refers to Jack's gang as a "fascist coup" and sees the opposition between democracy and totalitarianism as one of the novel's themes. The black garments and caps are, indeed, highly suggestive of the Nazi *Schutzstaffeln*, or SS—the "Black Angels" responsible for the Final Solution.

—P. Crawford (2002, p. 56)

Students can take these short, excerpted analyses and use them as starting points for examining the text. On the other hand, students' encounters with written criticism should not be limited to short excerpts like these. Have students (either with you, in small groups, or on their own) examine full texts of critical essays and then work those readings into their own writing in connection with the text. Chapter 8 of this book shares some resources that collect critical essays on the text. If time permits, you may even have students do what amounts to a literature review by reading several secondary source analyses of *Lord of the Flies* and identifying similarities or differences between them.

ACTIVITY (SAS #27): CRITICAL SOURCES

Have students find two critical essays related to *Lord of the Flies* in print or on the web and read them carefully. Then, using the first two columns of the worksheet, have students write main points from the essays, each in one column. In the third column, students are to write their own thoughts on the ideas presented in the two essays. Instruct them to identify points of overlap in the interpretations and points of possible difference or even disagreement; then, have them summarize their discoveries in a short paper.

Student critical writing, ultimately, is the outgrowth of a rigorous process of examining text. One role of literary criticism is to illuminate literary work. By virtue of the scholar's activity, we gain a deeper understanding and appreciation for a work, or we devalue the work as counter to contemporary pursuits, be they mental, emotional, political, or otherwise. Criticism at its best functions similarly to other kinds of scholarly activity, such as scientific research or spiritual and humanist philosophy, to help us understand ourselves through the literary expressions that are part of our cultural heritage.

Students gain important critical thinking skills by engaging in literary criticism, and it allows them to participate in a conversation that is greater than their individual selves, thus helping them to grow in inestimable ways. They may misfire when they attempt to place value on aspects of *Lord of the Flies* that they only partially understand or use critical lenses that they don't understand, but the process itself is vital, and you can easily show them that even published essays on *Lord of the Flies* reach sometimes questionable conclusions. I hope you will take the time to bring criticism into your unit on *Lord of the Flies*.

A Note on Creative Writing

Students can write creatively during their study of *Lord of the Flies* in ways that help them connect the novel to their lives and in ways that further their understanding of the work, as well as their own creative abilities. One way to get students engaged in creative writing is to have them imagine a different group of children on an island, perhaps themselves and their classmates. Have them write stories or scripts that depict what they think would happen in that circumstance. They could also maroon a group of children in a different setting, such as a burned out shopping mall or a typical school.

Martens-Baker (2009) discovered that combining online discussion between classes at different schools working collaboratively to understand *Lord of the Flies* led to creative work on "tribal paradise brochures." Allowing students to write songs, write scripts, create brochures, paint paintings, develop dance interpretation, or engage any of the arts (perhaps designing shelters?) gives them the opportunity to demonstrate what they know of the novel in untraditional forms that add value to the educational experience (Eisner, 1979; Duggan, 2007).

One idea that may be productive is to have students construct storyboards, as though they are going to render *Lord of the Flies* in graphic novel format. No graphic novel for *Lord of the Flies* exists (that I am aware of), and so you can sell the activity to your students with the possibility that their graphic novel will be the one that is published.

ACTIVITY (SAS #28): STORYBOARDING *LORD OF THE FLIES*

Have students take a chapter of *Lord of the Flies* or even one of the sections of a chapter (as identified in Chapter 4 of this book) and create a storyboard as though they are presenting the novel in graphic form. Have them create images that evoke the movement and the tone of the novel. Students can work together to produce the storyboard (this may also be a project option similar to those presented in Chapter 7 of this book). SAS #28 provides a starter format for panels in the storyboard.

Students can also write creative pieces or blogs examining the influence of *Lord of the Flies* in popular culture, including television shows like *Lost* and interpretations of the book in music.

DISCUSSION/JOURNAL TOPIC: *LORD OF THE FLIES* IN SONG: IRON MAIDEN VS. ELTON JOHN

Both the heavy metal band Iron Maiden (1995) and the British piano icon Elton John (1986) have written songs titled "Lord of the Flies." Both songs are readily accessible on YouTube, and the lyrics are available on several websites. Distribute or display the lyrics of the songs, play the songs for your students, and then ask them to discuss whether the artists captured the essence of the novel, or whether they took the concept in a different direction.

Students who have read, discussed, written, and performed in response to this novel will have a complete and rigorous educational experience. But to complete the circle of inquiry, small-group projects are a great way to culminate a unit, and that is the topic of Chapter 7.

Chapter Materials

Name: _____   Date: _____

Student Activity Sheet #20:
Character Intervention

Applicable Portion of the Novel: Individually chosen segments

Objectives:
1. Students will create a written script for a character intervention.
2. Students will interpret character conflict and motivation through writing.

Common Core Standard(s): RL.9-10.3 and W.9-10.1; RL.11-12.3 and W.11-12.1

Directions: Using your character charts (Student Activity Sheet #8), choose one character whose actions and situation you want to explore through writing. Using your charts and any other notes you've taken during reading, you can construct a visual diagnosis sheet with categories such as *biggest mistake*, *next likely move*, *potential protector(s)*, and *potential aggressor(s)*. Anticipating problems on the horizon for your character, write a summary, framed as a speech to be delivered at an "intervention" for that character. Identify the point in the novel where you would intervene for the character in order to prevent disaster. For example, an intervention with Roger may happen right before he rolls the rock onto Piggy, or perhaps earlier, when he is throwing rocks around Henry.

Sample character intervention script:

Character: Simon
Point at which the intervention takes place: Chapter 9

> Simon,
>
> I'm worried about you, and we need to talk right away. You showed great bravery by climbing the mountain, especially after that frightening interview with the pig's head, talking to you as though it were the Lord of the Flies. You have shown kindness to all you meet, especially Ralph, and you've tolerated the littluns as they follow you around. Most of all, you overcame your own disgust and vomiting to help untangle the poor, dead airman. I know you want to tell the others right away, but you might consider waiting until the storm passes. Jack and the others have shown little restraint when they have fresh meat to eat, and they may not recognize you if you come upon them suddenly . . .

Name: _____ Date: _____

Character intervention script draft:

Character: _____

Point at which the intervention takes place: _____

_____

_____

_____

_____

_____

_____

_____

_____

_____

_____

_____

_____

_____

_____

_____

_____

_____

_____

_____

_____

_____

_____

_____

_____

_____

_____

Student Activity Sheet #21:
Interactive News Report

Applicable Portion of the Novel: Individually chosen segments

Objectives:
1. Students will demonstrate reading comprehension through summary writing.
2. Students will develop skills in news writing and shared online response writing through comments on news stories.

Common Core Standard(s): RL.9-10.1, RL.9-10.2, and W.9-10.2; RL.11-12.1, RL.11-12.2, W.11-12.2, and W.11-12.3

Directions: Using the journalistic questions of what, who, when, where, how, and why, examine one important event from *Lord of the Flies* and generate a headline, a subhead, a lead (i.e., the first sentence in a news article), and a news story that you can present to your classmates in an online format. Your summary news article should catch the attention of your audience and capture the tone and importance of the event. Your fellow students can add blog-like comments in response to the news stories posted. The following is an example, created from the events of Chapter 4.

Headline: Ship Passes Island Unnoticed
Subhead: Signal fire allowed to go cold at critical time

Lead:

Several boys on the island noticed a ship passing on the horizon today, and in a stunning revelation, they found that the signal fire was allowed to go cold so that the assigned attendants of the fire could join in a pig hunt.

News Story:

When the boys noticed the ship, Ralph, the chief of the tribe, and several others raced to try to revive the fire but arrived too late. The ship passed on without noticing that the boys were on the island. Jack and his hunters, including Samneric, who were assigned to keep the fire going, returned to the scene of the fire with their first kill, a young pig. A loud confrontation between Ralph and Jack ensued, and when Piggy accused Jack of irresponsible behavior, Jack assaulted him and broke his glasses. Word is that a feast of pig followed. We will have more details as they are made available to us.

Post comments on this story:
1. tg.: It's a classic battle between the hunters and the domestic types.
2. g.c.: Piggy needs to learn not to confront Jack. He's a madman.
3. b.l.: I heard that Simon was crying, and that he offered his meat to Piggy at the feast.
4. z.d.: Would the ship have seen the fire anyway? Ralph should let it go.

Name: _____   Date: _____

News Report Draft

Headline: _____

Subhead: _____

Lead:

_____

_____

_____

News Story:

_____

_____

_____

_____

_____

_____

_____

_____

_____

_____

_____

_____

_____

_____

_____

_____

_____

Student Activity Sheet #22:
Title Defense

Applicable Portion of the Novel: All

Objectives:
1. Students will connect draft titles with story and theme in *Lord of the Flies*.
2. Students will be able to persuade an audience that one title is more appropriate than others.

Common Core Standard(s): RL.9-10.2, RL.9-10.10, and W.9-10.1; RL.11-12.3 and W.11-12.1

Directions: *Lord of the Flies* offers us an opportunity to examine how a book's title reflects the content, and how a title can be appropriate or inappropriate as a lure to potential readers. "Lord of the Flies" is not the first title that was considered for William Golding's first novel. Below is a list of other titles that were proposed, some by Golding himself and some by editors at his publishing house, Faber and Faber. All were ultimately rejected. Consider the titles, rank them in order of appropriateness, and then argue for your top choice as though you are part of the editorial team that is choosing the title.

Title	Rank
Strangers From Within	_____
A Cry of Children	_____
Nightmare Island	_____
This Island's Mine	_____
Beast in the Jungle	_____
An Island of Their Own	_____
Fun and Games	_____
The Isle Is Full of Noises	_____
To End an Island	_____

Defense of Top Choice:

_____

_____

_____

After you complete the activity, write a short reflection on why you think "Lord of the Flies," suggested by an editor at Faber and Faber named Alan Pringle, was chosen as the title, and whether that was a good choice, given the events, themes, and outcome of the novel.

_____

_____

_____

_____

Name: _____   Date: _____

Student Activity Sheet #23:
Pointing and Writing From a Line

Applicable Portion of the Novel: All

Objectives:
1. Students will pick significant lines from *Lord of the Flies* that illuminate the book's themes.
2. Students will participate in a shared reading of the text using chosen lines from class.
3. Students will be able to write an interpretive essay on *Lord of the Flies* using their chosen lines as starting points and support.

Common Core Standard(s): RL.9-10.1, RL.9-10.2, and RL.9-10.10; RL.11-12.1, W.11-12.1

Directions: Choose your favorite lines from *Lord of the Flies*, either from the Wall of Notable Quotes or from your own list. We will do a shared reading of those lines in class. Once we have read, choose one of the lines from your list or from the overall class list and use it as a starting point to write about the book as a whole. As you write your analysis, you are free to cite other lines that provide support for what you have to say about the book. We will share our writing in class.

Chosen Line:

_____

_____

Chapter and Page Number: _____

Analysis:

_____

_____

_____

_____

_____

_____

_____

_____

_____

_____

_____

Student Activity Sheet #24:
Sample Free-Response

Applicable Portion of the Novel: Chapter 9

Objectives:
1. Students will use literary elements to comprehend text.
2. Students will be able to write a convincing interpretation of character from a passage of complex text.

Common Core Standard(s): RL.9-10.1, RL.9-10.2, RL.9-10.5, and W.9-10.1; RL.11-12.3, RL.11-12.5, and W.11-12.1

Directions: In the following passage from *Lord of the Flies*, Simon awakes to find that he has had a fainting spell. In a well-written essay on a separate sheet of paper, explain how the author uses imagery to convey tone and reveal Simon's character.

With the running of the blood Simon's fit passed into the weariness of sleep. He lay in the mat of creepers while the evening advanced and the cannon continued to play. At last he woke and saw dimly the dark earth close by his cheek. Still he did not move, but lay there, his face sideways on the earth, his eyes looking dully before him. Then he turned over, drew his feet under him and laid hold of the creepers to pull himself up. When the creepers shook the flies exploded from the guts with a vicious note and clamped back on again. Simon got to his feet. The light was unearthly. The Lord of the Flies hung on his stick like a black ball.

Simon spoke aloud to the clearing.

"What else is there to do?"

Nothing replied. Simon turned away from the open space and crawled through the creepers till he was in the dusk of the forest. He walked drearily between the trunks, his face empty of expression, and the blood was dry round his mouth and chin. Only sometimes as he lifted the ropes of creeper aside and chose his direction from the trend of the land, he mouthed words that did not reach the air.

Presently the creepers festooned the trees less frequently and there was a scatter of pearly light from the sky down through the trees. This was the backbone of the island, the slightly higher land that lay beneath the mountain where the forest was no longer deep jungle. Here there were wide spaces interspersed with thickets and huge trees and the trend of the ground led him up as the forest opened. He pushed on, staggering sometimes with his weariness but never stopping. The usual brightness was gone from his eyes and he walked with a sort of glum determination like an old man. (p. 166–167)

Student Activity Sheet #25:
AP Free-Response Topics

Applicable Portion of the Novel: All

Objectives:
1. Students will be able to apply a statement about a particular literary theme or trope to *Lord of the Flies*.
2. Students will demonstrate comprehension of theme in *Lord of the Flies* in a well-organized, timed essay.
3. Students will gain confidence in their ability to write in response to AP essay topics.

Common Core Standard(s): RL.9-10.1-6 and W.9-10.1; RL.11-12.2 and W.11-12.1

Directions: Here are some example open topics that have been released by College Board. Choose one and follow the instructions, using *Lord of the Flies* as your text. You have 40 minutes.

From 2005—One of the strongest human drives seems to be a desire for power. Write an essay in which you discuss how a character in a novel or a drama struggles to free himself or herself from the power of others or seeks to gain power over others. Be sure to demonstrate in your essay how the author uses this power struggle to enhance the meaning of the work. (College Board, 2005b, p. 4)

From 2009—Many works of literature deal with political or social issues. Choose a novel or play that focuses on a political or social issue. Then write an essay in which you analyze how the author uses literary elements to explore this issue and explain how the issue contributes to the meaning of the work as a whole. Do not merely summarize the plot. (College Board, 2009, p. 4)

From 2010—The British novelist Fay Weldon offers this observation about happy endings: "The writers, I do believe, who get the best and most lasting response from readers are the writers who offer a happy ending through moral development. By a happy ending, I do not mean mere fortunate events—a marriage or a last-minute rescue from death—but some kind of spiritual reassessment or moral reconciliation, even with the self, even at death." Choose a novel or play that has the kind of ending Weldon describes. In a well-written essay, identify the "spiritual reassessment or moral reconciliation" evident in the ending and explain its significance in the work as a whole. (College Board 2010, p. 76)

From 2012—"And after all, our surroundings influence our lives and characters as much as fate, destiny or any supernatural agency," Pauline Hopkins, *Contending Forces*. Choose a novel or play in which cultural, physical, or geographical surroundings shape psychological or moral traits in a character. Then write a well-organized essay in which you analyze how surroundings affect this character and illuminate the meaning of the work as a whole. (College Board, 2012, p. 4)

Notes:

_____

_____

_____

Student Activity Sheet #26
Notes, Notes, Notes

Applicable Portion of the Novel: All

Objectives:
1. Students will engage the research-based techniques of note taking to build an interpretation of *Lord of the Flies*.
2. Students will organize notes from their study of the novel to construct a thesis-driven essay.

Common Core Standard(s): RL.9-10.2, RL.9-10.10, and W.9-10.1; RL.11-12.1, RL.11-12.2, and W.11-12.1

Directions: Review the notes and journal entries you have written in the process of reading and discussing *Lord of the Flies*, then draw some conclusions about the text. Consult your notes for thoughts and impressions that will lead to thesis statements about the novel. List possible thesis statements and then write a short critical essay that argues the validity of your thesis. In the conclusion to your essay, extend your thesis to argue its relevance or connection to contemporary culture.

Notes:

_____

_____

_____

_____

_____

_____

_____

_____

_____

_____

_____

_____

_____

_____

_____

_____

Student Activity Sheet #27
Critical Sources

Applicable Portion of the Novel: All

Objectives:
1. Students will incorporate secondary sources related to *Lord of the Flies* to build and clarify their interpretations of the book.
2. Students will demonstrate understanding of complex informative text by agreeing or disagreeing with critics' stances on *Lord of the Flies*.

Common Core Standard(s): RL.9-10.9, RI.9-10.1-3, and W.9-10.2; RL.9-10.7, RI.11-12.1, RI.11-12.7, and W.11-12.1

Directions: Find two critical essays related to *Lord of the Flies* in print or on the web and read them carefully. Then, using the chart provided, write main points from the essays in the first two columns. In the third column, write your own thoughts on the ideas presented in the two essays. Identify points of overlap in the interpretations and points of possible difference or even disagreement. Summarize your discoveries in a short paper.

Critical Sources Chart

Critical Essay #1	Critical Essay #2	My Thoughts:
Title: _____	Title: _____	
Author: _____	Author: _____	
Main Ideas:	**Main Ideas:**	

Name: _____   Date: _____

Student Activity Sheet #28:
Storyboarding *Lord of the Flies*

Applicable Portion of the Novel: Individually chosen segments

Objectives:
1. Students will translate a section of *Lord of the Flies* into a storyboard or graphic novel format.
2. Students will articulate choices in image and language to portray the story through their storyboard.

Common Core Standard(s): RL.9-10.1-3 and RL.9-10.7; RL.9-10.5, RL.11-12.7, and RL.11-12.9

Directions: Take a chapter of *Lord of the Flies* or even one of the sections of a chapter that we have discussed in class and create a storyboard as though you are presenting the novel in graphic form. Create images that evoke the movement and the tone of the novel.

Name: _____

Date: _____

Storyboard Template

Advanced Placement Classroom: Lord of the Flies © Prufrock Press • This page may be photocopied or reproduced with permission for single classroom use.

"Sharpen a stick at both ends": Project Ideas for *Lord of the Flies*

What will change your *Lord of the Flies* unit from a good one to a great one will be independent small-group projects that allow differentiation by interest and real inquiry, leading to student-to-student teaching and culminating activities that create a whole that is greater than the sum of its parts. As Blau (2003) stated, the best way to teach is to get students to do the work that we do to prepare to teach. Students take the initiative and the responsibility to answer deep essential questions posed by themselves and by you, based on the themes in the text. I suggest you assign students to small groups (3–4 students, or perhaps even pairs) shortly after your class has completed a first read-through of the text. You may use the suggested inquiry topics here and/or generate your own with your students. Try to match student interest to the inquiry topic for greater engagement.

Give students 2–3 weeks to research their topics and create a multimedia teaching tool that presents answers to the essential questions with which they began. That research can happen concurrently with discussion/performance/writing activities in class (see Chapters 5–6). Have students present their inquiry findings in class, using the presentations as a vehicle for teaching good speaking and listening skills. How you fit these inquiry projects into your unit, and how they complement other assessments, will be up to you, but I include a sample rubric at the end of this chapter as a model for how you might assess group efforts. I suggest that you use these projects as an opportunity to do information literacy teaching with your students, and that you invite your school's librarian to work with students on intelligent use of electronic search engines. You may teach students how to discriminate between reliable and unreliable sources.

Here are some suggested avenues for inquiry, including descriptions, sets of essential questions, and resources to begin the inquiry.

Bullying

Students who react viscerally to the treatment of Piggy and, to some extent, Simon and the littluns, may want to investigate the theme of bullying as an ongoing problem in contemporary society. Golding's portrayal of the casual exclusion of Piggy from the community, along with the overt violence toward him shown by Jack and Roger, leave us with deep questions about how children treat one another. For students wishing to examine bullying in contemporary culture, there are a number of resources and networks that can provide statistics, strategies, and support.

Possible questions include

- Is Golding's portrayal of bullying in *Lord of the Flies* an accurate depiction of the intimidation practices used by child bullies?

- How have children changed since the 1950s in regards to bullying?

- What forms does bullying take today? How can it be prevented?

- What does the word "empathy" mean, and what does it look like in action?

Students may want to look at

- *English Journal* (July, 2012), Volume 101, Issue 6

- http://www.stopbullying.gov

- http://www.pacer.org/bullying

- http://www.bullyingprevention.org

- http://www.itgetsbetter.org

- *The Chocolate War* by Robert Cormier

- *Thirteen Reasons Why* by Jay Asher

The Coral Island, Treasure Island, and Swallows and Amazons

This inquiry looks at boys' adventure stories that were popular in England in the 19th and 20th centuries. Students may either split duties and read one of these texts individually or they may read the same text as a group with the idea of constructing parallels with *Lord of the Flies*. (*The Coral Island* would be the best book to choose if the group decides to read just one.)

Possible questions include

- What events and scenes in the earlier adventure tales are recreated in some way in *Lord of the Flies*?

- What similarities and differences exist between the individual characters of the same names in *The Coral Island* and *Lord of the Flies*?

- How has Golding changed the themes presented in the earlier adventure stories? What is he saying about those stories?

Students may want to look at

- *The Coral Island* by R. M. Ballantyne

- *Treasure Island* by Robert Louis Stevenson

- *Swallows and Amazons* by Arthur Ransome (Book 1)

Behind the Mask

Students who are interested in investigating the phenomenon of how wearing a mask or otherwise hiding one's face leads to loss of inhibition against violent behavior may find that significant work has been done in this area. Philip Zimbardo's Stanford Prison Experiment and his book, *The Lucifer Effect,* connect a sense of anonymity with violence, as demonstrated at Abu Ghraib by U.S. military personnel. Zimbardo often cites *Lord of the Flies* as the prototype for how wearing a mask frees people from inhibition against committing violent acts. Students can start by identifying specific statements in *Lord of the Flies* that connect the wearing of paint with freedom from self-consciousness.

Possible questions include

- What effect does painting one's face or wearing a mask have on our ability to commit acts of violence?

- What examples exist that demonstrate the effects of anonymity on behavior?

Students may want to look at

- The Stanford prison experiment, the Milgram experiment

- *The Lucifer Effect* by Philip Zimbardo

- *The Mask* comic books by John Arcudi and Doug Mahnke

The Heart of Darkness: Exploration of Human Nature

Students who want to examine the book's commentary on human nature are encouraged to investigate different philosophical and/or religious stances on the nature of humankind, with the goal of developing their own ideas. As the director of these inquiry projects, you will need to show respect for and sensitivity to the students' cultural and religious backgrounds, and communication with parents may be necessary to avoid possible conflict.

Possible questions include

- Is humanity essentially good or evil?

- What is necessary to prevent people from killing each other?

Students may want to look at

- *Leviathan* by Thomas Hobbes

- *The Social Contract* by Jean-Jacques Rousseau

- *Heart of Darkness* by Joseph Conrad

Democracy and Dictatorship

Students who wish to see Ralph's and Jack's different societies as echoes of larger political structures may wish to examine the political aspects of democracy versus authoritarian rule as imposed by a dictator. Students may look at classical democracies, such as ancient Greece, and contemporary democracies, as well as the rules of famous dictators.

Possible questions include

- What are the social advantages of having one ruler?

- What is the difference between the concept of the benevolent ruler and the despot?

- How do democracies work, and what makes them difficult to maintain?

- What leads the democracy in *Lord of the Flies* to turn to violent dictatorship?

Students may want to look at

- The Declaration of Independence

- *The Dictator's Handbook: Why Bad Behavior is Almost Always Good Politics* by Bruce Bueno de Mesquita
- *Dictatorship vs. Democracy: Terrorism and Communism* by Leon Trotsky

WWII and Cold War History

The two brief references to nuclear war in the book may lead students to want to investigate the Cold War between the United States and its allies (including Great Britain) and the Soviet Union in the 1950s–1980s. Understanding the atrocities committed during World War II and the threat of nuclear annihilation that existed (and still exists) following the war will help students to understand how the society of the boys on the island may represent a childish parallel to the world of the adults.

Possible questions include
- How is *Lord of the Flies* informed by the politics of the time during which Golding wrote it?
- How does *Lord of the Flies* echo human behavior exhibited during World War II?
- What is the significance of The Cold War in Golding's novel?

Students may want to look at
- *Wartime: Understanding and Behavior in the Second World War* by Paul Fussell
- *The Cold War: A Very Short Introduction* by Robert J. McMahon

Golding's Life

The biography of the author is always a good resource for information that may deepen our understanding of and appreciation for a work of literature. Golding was a Navy captain in WWII who saw extensive combat action, and a schoolmaster at Bishop Wordsworth School for several years. He had seen the atrocities of the war, and he knew a great deal about boys and how they behave. He also commented frequently on what in his experience led him to write *Lord of the Flies*.

Possible questions include
- What events in William Golding's life may have shaped his ideas about humanity as presented in *Lord of the Flies*?

- What sources of knowledge did Golding have access to that would give him authority to write the book?

- What are the limits to which understanding Golding's life story serves us in developing our own interpretations of his novel?

Students may want to look at
- *William Golding* by John Carey
- *A Moving Target* by William Golding

Children of War

Often forgotten in discussions of war are the children, and how war affects their lives. Not only is their survival at stake, but their social and psychological development and their ability to function are impaired, sometimes profoundly, even though media explorations of children of war often transform them into superheroes, perhaps a favorite fantasy of the children themselves. Students who want to bring a fresh perspective to their study of *Lord of the Flies* may wish to explore the story from the standpoint that these boys, even though all of them but Piggy seem oblivious to it, are war refugees, abandoned by the great conflict that goes on in the world that has forgotten them.

Possible questions include
- What is known about the psychological and social effects of war on children?

- How do the boys in *Lord of the Flies* reflect typical symptoms of children of war?

- What can be done to help children of war?

Students may want to look at
- UNICEF
- *Children of War*, a film by Brian Single
- *Children of War: Fighting, Dying, Surviving*, a radio program by KQED

Reality TV and Conflict

For over 25 seasons, *Survivor* on CBS has captivated a certain segment of the population with a staged "war" between competing groups of adults in an exotic, wild, and often island environment. One could almost say that the show is a direct descendent of Golding's book. But *Survivor* was only the beginning, as reality television has become, for a variety of factors, the dominant programming format on network and cable TV. Even attempts to bake cupcakes can be transformed into blood sport.

Possible questions include

- What accounts for the popularity of *Survivor* and other reality television shows that present conflict between people?

- What qualities in the contestants do viewers enjoy watching, and how do these qualities compare to the qualities exhibited by the boys in *Lord of the Flies*?

Students may want to look at

- Episodes of *Survivor* on CBS

- *Tribal Warfare:* Survivor *and the Political Unconscious of Reality Television* by Christopher J. Wright

Humans and Ecology: Burning Forests

The destruction of the island in *Lord of the Flies* has been likened to the turning of heaven into hell, as the book is rich with symbolism. But a contemporary reader may examine the boys' abuse of nature from the very beginning. The landing of the plane is described as a "scar" on the island (p. 1). The boys indiscriminately foul their water supply with their own excretions, they kill the pigs on the island with increased frequency, and they even topple the rocks from the outcropping at the end of the island. Most egregiously, they set the island on fire twice, the second time burning it completely. Students may use such a reading to examine environmental ethos and the problem of rainforest destruction.

Possible questions include

- How is *Lord of the Flies* emblematic of human destruction of the environment?

- What are the dangers associated with a dominance ethos with regard to the environment?

Students may want to look at

- The *National Geographic* website (specifically, http://environment.nationalgeographic.com/environment/habitats/rainforest-threats/)

- Foundation for Deep Ecology (http://www.deepecology.org)

Critical Theory and *Lord of the Flies*: Freudian, Marxist, Christian, and Feminist Readings

Lord of the Flies not only provides a great opportunity for students to examine stock literary elements such as symbol, foreshadowing, and metaphor, but it also provides a good way to introduce students to critical theory and different critical "lenses" through which a book may be interpreted. Students may choose different perspectives to examine and, having learned aspects of those critical lenses, apply them to the novel.

Possible questions include

- How do different critical lenses affect our understanding of *Lord of the Flies*?

- How can specific critical lenses be applied to *Lord of the Flies*, and what details or events from the book come to the forefront under these different lenses?

Students may want to look at

- *Critical Encounters in the English Classroom: Teaching Literary Theory to Adolescents (2nd Edition)* by Deborah Appleman

- *Doing Literary Criticism: Helping Students Engage with Challenging Texts* by Tim Gillespie

The Inheritors or Other Golding Books

Following the success of *Lord of the Flies*, Golding enjoyed a long and productive career as a writer, leading to his receiving the Nobel Prize in Literature in 1983. The two books that immediately followed *Lord of the Flies*, *The Inheritors* (1955) and *Pincher Martin* (1956), deal with similar themes as *Lord of the Flies* and feature similar techniques of deep description, character development, and a reversal of perspective at the end. Students can further explore Golding's philosophy through reading these books and connecting them to *Lord of the Flies*.

Possible questions include

- What themes in *The Inheritors* and/or *Pincher Martin* are similar to the themes in *Lord of the Flies*?

- How do *The Inheritors* and/or *Pincher Martin* address the nature of man?

- What techniques of author's craft does Golding employ to develop *The Inheritors* and/or *Pincher Martin*?

Students may want to look at

- *The Inheritors* by William Golding

- *Pincher Martin* by William Golding

- *Of Earth and Darkness: The Novels of William Golding* by Arnold Johnston (or the many other collections of essays on Golding's work; see Chapter 8 for other titles)

Maslow's Hierarchy of Needs

Following from the prereading activity described in Chapter 3, interested students can investigate Maslow's theory in depth and do a structural analysis of *Lord of the Flies* using Maslow's hierarchy of needs as the basis for interpreting character actions and story outcomes.

Possible questions include

- How does viewing *Lord of the Flies* through the lens of Maslow's hierarchy of needs affect our interpretation of the novel?

- What levels on the hierarchy do different characters achieve at different points in the story? How do those levels come into conflict with each other?

Students may want to look at

- *Motivation and Personality* by Abraham Maslow, Robert Frager, and James Fadiman

Film and Stage

Lord of the Flies has been adapted twice into full-length feature films: once in the early 1960s and again in 1990. The mid-1990s also saw the production of Nigel Williams's adaptation of the book at the Royal Shakespeare Theatre in Stratford. These films and the script of the play are available for use in the classroom.

Possible questions include

- How do the film and theatre adaptations treat the central themes of Golding's book? How are they faithful to the book, and how do they change elements of the book to suit a different medium?

- How do the films or the play/scripts further illuminate *Lord of the Flies*?

Students may want to look at

- *Lord of the Flies*, a film directed by Peter Brook

- *Lord of the Flies*, a film directed by Harry Hook
- *William Golding's* Lord of the Flies: *Acting Edition*, a stage adaptation written by Nigel Williams

The British School System

The boys in *Lord of the Flies* are products of a British school system that saw itself as the best in the world, and which bred a spirit of domination in the children, as Jack illustrates when he says, "We're English, and the English are best at everything" (p. 44). But the social structure of boys' schools, with the strict rules and the repressive hierarchy, led to similar hierarchies among the boys themselves. Golding taught in one of these schools for years.

Possible questions include

- What were British boys' schools like in the 1940s and 1950s?

- How was the violence of fighting and bullying addressed or not addressed?

- What were the common rules in these schools?

Students may want to look at

- *Understanding* Lord of the Flies: *A Student Casebook to Issues, Sources, and Historical Documents* by Kirstin Olsen

Rubric for Evaluation of Group Inquiry Projects

This is a general rubric, so point values are not included. Adapt it to suit your needs in evaluating your students.

Category	Excellent	Good	Fair	Poor
Clarity of focus	Inquiry questions are well formed and lead to authentic investigation. Questions may evolve during investigation.	Inquiry questions are clear and open ended. Questions may change as research progresses.	Inquiry questions are related to inquiry topic. Questions are rigid and not adaptable to new findings.	Inquiry questions lack focus.
Demonstration of knowledge	Group presents findings in a way that allows fellow students to learn. Information is extensive and verifiable. Conclusions are logical and defensible.	Group presents findings that demonstrate knowledge gained in relation to research questions. Information presented is substantial, and conclusions are reasonable.	Group presents findings that show considerable effort. Information is verifiable but not extensive. Conclusions are vague.	Group does not present substantial information or learning and reaches questionable conclusions.
Connection of knowledge gained to novel	Connection of conclusions regarding inquiry questions and *Lord of the Flies* is clear and extensive. Inquiry serves to illuminate the novel.	Connection of knowledge gained to novel is clear and reasonable. Group answers to inquiry questions are clear and supported.	Connection of knowledge gained to novel is present but not clearly delineated.	Connection to Novel is unclear and may not be reasonable.

Category	Excellent	Good	Fair	Poor
Group cohesion	Group works together without serious conflict. Every group member contributes and takes responsibility for group success.	Group works together well in general and everyone takes an active role. Conflict is settled and overcome.	Group lacks cohesiveness but manages to work through differences. Majority of group members take active role.	Group does not work together. Individual members either take on too much or too little of work. Work does not get done.
Individual contributions to group	Pulled weight, took initiative, worked well with others, and helped all to succeed.	Pulled weight in group and made contribution. Worked well with others.	Completed work within the group but did not lead or do as much as other members. Caused conflict with other group members.	Did not participate at an acceptable level.
Multimedia presentation	Presentation exploits media format to full effect, allows learner access to all information. Graphics and media element enhance learning.	Presentation is accessible and clear, demonstrating inquiry findings in way that is easily digestible. Links work.	Presentation format ineffective for demonstrating knowledge gained and connection to novel. Information is present but not easy to navigate.	Media element is poorly conceived and executed. Information is not easily accessible or missing.
In-class presentation	All group members present in clear, consistent voices with good eye contact. Language is clear, use of media aids is appropriate. Stays within time limit.	All group members contribute and share time in a well-organized presentation that makes good use of media aids and stays within time limit.	All members participate and presentation demonstrates the findings in the media element. Some findings may be unclear due to poor organization.	Presentation skills are lacking—poor eye contact, uneven contributions, and thin content.

"How many of you are there?": Resources for Teaching *Lord of the Flies*

What follows is a list of resources that have been helpful to me in writing this book and that I can recommend to you as having value toward increasing your understanding and appreciation for *Lord of the Flies* and your ability to teach it well. These works also appear in the References section of this book, but they are highlighted here in several categories to help you decide which works most fit your own educational goals. That being said, you may also find materials of value to you listed in the References section that are not listed here.

Books About William Golding

- *Talk: Conversations with William Golding* by Jack I. Biles

- *William Golding: The Man Who Wrote* Lord of the Flies by John Carey

Collections of Essays on Golding's Fiction

- *William Golding* (Revised Edition; Twayne's English Authors Series) by Bernard F. Dick

- *The Modern Allegories of William Golding* by Larry L. Dickson

- *Politics and History in William Golding: The World Turned Upside Down* by Paul Crawford

- *William Golding: Literature and Life* by Lawrence S. Friedman

- *William Golding* (Modern Novelists Series) by James Jack Gindin

- *Of Earth and Darkness: The Novels of William Golding* by Arnold Johnston

- *William Golding: A Critical Study* by James R. Baker

- *The Art of William Golding* by Bernard S. Oldsey and Stanley Weintraub
- *William Golding: A Structural Reading of His Fiction* by Philip Redpath
- *The Void and the Metaphors: A New Reading of William Golding's Fiction* by Yasunori Sugmiura
- *William Golding: The Dark Fields of Discovery* by Virginia Tiger

Collections of Essays on Golding's Fiction (Multiple Authors)
- *Critical Essays on William Golding*, edited by James R. Baker
- *William Golding: Some Critical Considerations*, edited by Jack I. Biles and Robert O. Evans
- *The Novels of William Golding*, edited by S. J. Boyd

Essays on *Lord of the Flies*
- *William Golding's* Lord of the Flies (Bloom's Modern Critical Interpretations) by Harold Bloom
- *William Golding's* Lord of the Flies: *A Source Book* by Francis William Nelson
- Lord of the Flies: *Fathers and Sons* (Twayne's Masterwork Studies) by Patrick Reilly

Teaching Guides
- *William Golding's* Lord of the Flies (Bloom's Guides), edited by Harold Bloom
- The Lord of the Flies: *A Teaching Guide* by Mary Elizabeth Podhaizer
- *Lord of the Flies: Casebook Edition* by William Golding, edited by James R. Baker and Arthur P. Ziegler, Jr.
- *Understanding* Lord of the Flies: *A Student Casebook to Issues, Sources, and Historical Documents* by Kirstin Olsen

Related Novels
- *The Coral Island: A Tale of the Pacific Ocean* by R. M. Ballantyne
- *Pincher Martin* by William Golding
- *The Inheritors* by William Golding

Movies
- *Lord of the Flies* (1963), directed by Peter Brook

☙ *Lord of the Flies* (1990), directed by Harry Hook

Dramatic Script

 ☙ *William Golding's* Lord of the Flies: *Acting Edition* by Nigel Williams

Online Resources

 ☙ William Golding (official website; http://www.william-golding.co.uk)

 ☙ *Lord of the Flies* Video SparkNote (http://www.sparknotes.com/sparknotes/video/flies)

Note: A Google search of "Lord of the Flies" will turn up millions of hits. Virtually every teacher lesson clearinghouse has materials related to the book, and there are CliffsNotes, SparkNotes, Schmoop guides, and everything from YouTube videos (a great resource for amateur dramatic productions) to analytical papers available for purchase with just a click of a mouse. The websites above are my recommendations for trusted, reliable, and, in the case of the latter, entertaining information.

Bullying Resources

 ☙ *English Journal*, July 2012, Volume 101, Issue 6.

 ☙ StopBullying.gov (http://www.stopbullying.gov)

 ☙ Pacer's National Bullying Prevention Center (http://www.pacer.org/bullying)

 ☙ Bullying Prevention Resource Guide (http://www.bullyingprevention.org)

 ☙ It Gets Better Project (http://www.itgetsbetter.org)

Other

 ☙ *The Lucifer Effect* by Philip Zimbardo

References

Allen, L. M. (Producer), & Brook, P. (Director). (1963). *Lord of the Flies* [Motion picture]. United Kingdom: British Lion.

Allen, L. M. (Producer), & Hook, H. (Director). (1990). *Lord of the Flies* [Motion picture]. United States: Columbia Pictures.

Applebee, A., & Langer, J. (2011). A snapshot of writing instruction in middle schools and high schools. *English Journal, 100*(6), 14–27.

Appleman, D. (2000). *Critical encounters in high school English: Teaching literary theory to adolescents.* New York, NY: Teachers College Press.

Ballantyne, R. M. (1858, 1990). *The coral island: A tale of the Pacific Ocean.* Oxford, England: Oxford University Press.

Baker, J. R. (Ed.) (1988). *Critical essays on William Golding.* Boston, MA: G.K. Hall.

Baker, J. R. (1963, 1988). Why it's no go. In J. R. Baker (Ed.), *Critical essays on William Golding* (pp. 22–31). Boston, MA: G.K. Hall.

Biles, J. I. (1970). *Talk: Conversations with William Golding.* New York, NY: Harcourt Brace Jovanovich, Inc.

Biles, J. I., & Evans, R. O. (Eds.). *William Golding: Some critical considerations.* Lexington: University of Kentucky Press.

Blau, S. D. (2003). *The literature workshop: Teaching texts and their readers.* Portsmouth, NH: Heinemann.

Bloom, H. (Ed.). (2004). *Bloom's Guides: William Golding's* Lord of the Flies. Philadelphia, PA: Chelsea House.

Bloom, H. (Ed.). (1999). *Modern critical interpretations: William Golding's* Lord of the Flies. New York, NY: Infobase.

Bloom, H. (Ed.). (2008). *Modern critical interpretations: William Golding's* Lord of the Flies. New York, NY: Infobase.

Boal, A. (2002). *Games for actors and non-actors* (2nd ed.). New York, NY: Routledge.

Boeree, C. G. (2006). *Abraham Maslow.* Retrieved from http://webspace.ship. edu/cgboer/maslow.html

Boyd, S. J. (1988). *The novels of William Golding.* Sussex, England: The Harvester Press.

Buck, A. (2012). Examining digital literacy practices on social network sites. *Research in the Teaching of English, 47,* 9–38.

Carey, J. (2009). *William Golding: The man who wrote* Lord of the Flies. London, England: Faber and Faber.

College Board. (2005a). *AP® English composition and literature 2005 free-response questions.* Retrieved from http://apcentral.collegeboard.com/apc/ public/repository/_ap05_frq_englishlit_45549.pdf

College Board. (2005b). *AP® English composition and literature 2005 free-response questions (Form B).* Retrieved from http://apcentral.collegeboard. com/apc/public/repository/_ap05_frq_englishlit__45550.pdf

College Board. (2009). *2009 AP® English composition and literature free-response questions (Form B).* Retrieved from http://apcentral.collegeboard.com/apc/ public/repository/ap09_frq_english_literature_formb.pdf

College Board. (2011a). *English literature.* Retrieved from http://www. collegeboard.com/student/testing/ap/sub_englit.html?englit

College Board. (2012). *AP English literature and composition 2012 free-response questions.* Retrieved from http://apcentral.collegeboard.com/apc/public/ repository/ap_2012_frq_eng_lit.pdf

College Board. (2011b). *Study skills: Writing.* Retrieved from http://www. collegeboard.com/student/testing/ap/english_lit/writing.html?englit

Common Core State Standards Initiative. (2012). *English Language Arts Standards.* Retrieved from http://www.corestandards.org/ELA-Literacy

Crawford, P. (2002). *Politics and history in William Golding: The world turned upside down.* Columbia: University of Missouri Press.

Delbaere-Garant, J. (1978). Rhythm and expansion in *Lord of the Flies.* In J. I. Biles & R. O. Evans (Eds.), *William Golding: Some critical considerations,* 72–86. Lexington: University of Kentucky Press.

Dewey, J. (1938). *Experience and Education.* New York, NY: Simon & Schuster.

Dick, B. F. (1987). *William Golding* (Revised edition). Boston, MA: Twayne.

Dickson, L. L. (1990). *The modern allegories of William Golding.* Tampa: University of South Florida Press.

Duggan, T. J. (2007). Ways of knowing: Exploring artistic representations of concepts. *Gifted Child Today, 30*(4), 56–63.

Education: Lord of the campus. (1962, June 22). *TIME*. Retrieved from http://www.time.com/time/magazine/article/0,9171,869976,00.html

Eisner, E. (1979). *The educational imagination*. Upper Saddle River, NJ: Merrill/Prentice Hall.

Eisner, E. (2001). What does it mean to say a school is doing well? *Phi Delta Kappan, 82,* 367–372.

Elizabeth, M. (1999). The Lord of the Flies: *A teaching guide*. New York, NY: Riverhead Books.

Epstein, E. L. (1997). Notes on *Lord of the Flies*. In W. Golding, *Lord of the flies* (pp. 237–242). New York, NY: Riverhead.

Frängsmyr, T., & Allén, S. (Eds.). (1993). *Nobel lectures, Literature 1981–1990*. Singapore: World Scientific.

Friedman, L. S. (1993). *William Golding*. New York, NY: Continuum.

Gillespie, T. (2010). *Doing literary criticism: Helping students engage with challenging texts*. Portland, ME: Stenhouse.

Gindin, J. (1988). *Modern novelists: William Golding*. New York, NY: St. Martin's.

Golden, J. (2001). *Reading in the dark: Using film as a tool in the English classroom*. Urbana, IL: NCTE.

Golding, W. (1982). *A moving target*. New York, NY: Farrar Straus Giroux.

Golding, W. (1954, 1997). Lord of the flies: *Riverhead trade paperback edition*. New York, NY: Riverhead.

Golding, W. (1954, 1988). Lord of the flies: *Casebook edition* (J. R. Baker & A.P P. Ziegler, Jr. Eds.). New York, NY: Perigree.

Golding, W. (1956). *Pincher Martin*. London, England: Faber and Faber.

Golding, W. (1955). *The inheritors*. New York, NY: Harcourt, Brace & World.

Graham, S., & Perin, D. (2007). *Writing next: Effective strategies to improve writing of adolescents in middle and high schools*. New York: Carnegie Corporation.

Harris, S., & Gers, J. (1995). Lord of the flies [Recorded by Iron Maiden]. On *The X Factor* [CD]. London, England: EMI.

Hicks, T. (2009). *The digital writing workshop*. Portsmouth, NH: Heinemann.

John, E., & Taupin, B. (1986). Lord of the flies [Recorded by Elton John]. On B-Side to Slow rivers [Single record]. London, England: Big Pig Music.

Johnston, A. (1980). *Of Earth and darkness: The novels of William Golding*. Columbia: University of Missouri Press.

Kinkead-Weekes, M., & Gregor, I. (1967). *William Golding: A critical study*. London, England: Faber and Faber.

Langer, J. A. (2000). *Beating the odds: Teaching middle and high school students to read and write well* (2nd ed.). Albany, NY: National Research Center on English Learning and Achievement.

Marzano, R. J., Pickering, D. J., & Pollock, J.E. (2001). *Classroom instruction that works: Research-based strategies for increasing student achievement.* Alexandria, VA: ASCD.

Martens-Baker, S. (2009). Fantasy island meets the real world: Using online discussion forums in collaborative learning. *English Journal, 98*(5), 88–94.

Maslow, A., Frager, R., & Fadiman, J. (1987). *Motivation and personality* (3rd ed.). New York, NY: Harper Collins.

Murray, D. (2004). *Write to learn* (8th ed.). Belmont, CA: Heinle.

Neal, M. (2008). Look who's talking: Discourse analysis, discussion, and initiation-response-evaluation patterns in the college classroom. *Teaching in the Two-Year College, 53,* 272–281.

Nelson, W. (1963). *William Golding's* Lord of the Flies: *A sourcebook.* New York, NY: Odyssey.

Oldsey, B. S., & Weintraub, S. (1965). *The art of William Golding.* New York, NY: Harcourt, Brace, & World.

Olsen, K. (2000). *Understanding* Lord of the Flies: *A student casebook to issues, sources, and historical documents.* Westport, CT: Greenwood.

Raphael, T. E. (1986). Teaching question-answer relationships. *Reading Teacher, 39,* 516–520.

Redpath, P. (1986). *William Golding: A structural reading of his fiction.* London, England: Vision.

Reilly, P. (1992). Lord of the Flies: *Fathers and sons.* New York, NY: Twayne.

Rosenblatt, L. (1983). *Literature as exploration.* New York, NY: Noble & Noble.

Sugimura, Y. (2008). *The void and the metaphors: A new reading of William Golding's fiction.* Oxford, UK: Peter Lang.

Tiger, V. (1974). *William Golding: The dark fields of discovery.* London, England: Calder & Boyers.

Williams, N. (1996). *William Golding's Lord of the Flies: Acting edition.* London, England: Faber and Faber.

Zimbardo, P. (2007). *The Lucifer effect.* New York, NY: Random House.

About the Author

*T*imothy J. Duggan, Ed.D., works in the Department of Educational Inquiry and Curriculum Studies at Northeastern Illinois University in Chicago, where he teaches English education courses and conducts faculty development workshops for Chicago area teachers. This is Dr. Duggan's third book in the Prufrock Press series of Teaching Success Guides for the Advanced Placement Classroom. He lives in Skokie, IL, with his wife, Heidi, and his two children, Eamon and Liesel. He is also a performing singer-songwriter.